"Great bo ... errific, practical tips for p ... with age, both inside an...

Randy Gage, ... ng author of 'Risky is the New Safe' and 'Mad Genius'

"Our one-to-one coaching sessions began a year ago and I feel so far away from the person I was then. There's been a gradual awakening of the less-than-healthy daily routines which I hadn't initially realised were holding me back from being the person I'm moving towards today.

I was standing in the way of my own success and happiness before, but Tristan has helped me realise that anything is possible over time, with seemingly small, yet significant shifts in habits.

This book should be on the shelves of everyone committed to making changes for the better in their lives."

Karen Bianco, 58, Hartlepool

"I have watched Tristan's journey from him realising how he has helped himself to live his very best life, as the finest version of himself, to him realising that he had a chance to make a significant impact on other lives too.

Not only does he look fantastic for his age through an acceptance of self-love, he's then realised the significant psychological and mental benefits that have helped him live a happy, content, empowered and vibrant life. There's no place for jealousy as he is clearly committed to helping guys and girls of any age understand that they still matter and become the very best example of ourselves.

It gives me great pride to see my best buddy impacting so many lives and helping people look and feel great about themselves, and achieving the mental peace and calm that they'll inevitably get from having that support and non judgemental encouragement. The success stories that have come from those who follow him online, and the results from those he works with one-to-one, means he's already quite literally changed a lot of family trees.

I'm excited to see him release this book and believe that the more people that read this and follow Tristan online who then act upon the guidance and support, the greater chance we have of achieving happier and healthier lives."
Wes Linden, Amazon best-seller and International Speaker, London

"If you're looking for the secret to longevity, eternal youth and feeling full of energy every day, then look no further than Tristan 'Peter Pan' Lee for inspiration and practical tried and tested advice."
Chris Williams, 59, Author of 'Don't Just Dream It, Do It!', Birmingham

"I had the joy of working with Tristan recently through my KAPOW! programme, and if there is anyone you should be following on social media that will help you be the best you that you can be, it's him. Read this now - you won't regret it!"
Sheena Whyatt, Lincolnshire

"I've been working with Tristan for nine months now as one of his one-to-one clients, and all I can say is a huge THANK YOU!

We started when I was struggling with very low self-esteem and low self-confidence after a marriage break-up. We have focused on food, fitness and feelings, and all I can say is WOW! Tristan's empathy is amazing and I can honestly say he has totally changed my direction in life.

He's helped me improve my lifestyle with lots of small changes over a period of time. My weight is reducing steadily and my self-confidence is growing by the day.

This book will become a must-have for anyone wanting to age with attitude."
Gary Murray, 46, Bury St. Edmunds

"Tristan Lee has been an inspirational coach! He gets his message across in a fun and sensitive way and is someone who really listens to your individual needs. As someone who has taken on a plant-based approach to food, Tristan has helped me develop an amazing repertoire of recipes which provide all my nutritional requirements, and has helped me to lose over three stone (approximately 20kg) in weight and get back into the best shape of my life.

He's simply amazing and choosing to work with him on a one-to-one basis was one of my best decisions yet, and this book will help others transform their life too."
Derek Thomas, 56, Cardiff, Wales

"Tristan's positive messages have helped highlight the best of myself, which has been great for me as I have some health challenges.

I think everyone should follow Tristan for the love that he shares and read this book from front to back."
Chris Kazama Morris, 28, Paisley, Scotland

"Tristan's book will change your life! You'll have a huge insight into how to maintain a healthy lifestyle and a variety of foods that will help you. I thoroughly enjoyed his workshops, we had a lot of fun and had a better insight into how to make better choices day-to-day."
James Thomas, 20, Wales

"The problem with huge, life-changing goals is their size, and if you've never previously achieved such a mind-boggling goal it can seem too big a task to even get started!

Tristan helps you to break down your goals into a series of daily decisions to move gradually towards them, by taking into account your feelings towards yourself and your goal. He helps you feel great about yourself even on the days that you've stepped off from your path. He makes it okay for you to be you!

Tristan has helped me feel great about being me even on those days that haven't gone to plan! His approach is informative, fun and spot on. This book will leave you feeling empowered, inspired, focused and gorgeous."
Glynnis Wisbey, Ashford, Kent

"Tristan is a constant inspiration in my daily effort to keep on track with daily exercise, while eating great-tasting, healthy food!

Tristan's 'slight edge' approach with the emphasis on long-term plans to look fab and feel great (inside and out) is surely the way forward. Fitness should not be for summer, but for life!

Thank you, Tristan, for your awesome, positive tips on fitness training, nutrition and fashion! This book will help you learn first-hand how to look and feel gorgeous!"
David Long, 48, Celebrity Photographer, Midlands

"Attending one of Tristan's Gorgeousness Roadshows was an absolute privilege and delight. A truly fabulous speaker - Tristan delivers with know-how, absolute sincerity and an abundance of delectable humour.

I came away inspired to become the very best version of me, and to encourage others to do the same. His simple

message of 'you are enough' powered through for me. This book is a must-read."
Katie Nell, Saffron Walden, Essex

"Tristan has a contagious, magical quality born from personal challenges.

His courage to face those challenges, his perseverance and persistence in the face of adversity is inspiring.

His caring and empathetic nature, sparky sense of humour and generous personality motivates others to find ways to feel good about themselves every day. This book is going to help a lot of people."
Katherine Morgan, 48, Wendover, Hertfordshire

Ageing doesn't have to be doom and gloom!

MUNCH, MOVE, moisturise!

How to age **gorgeously** in your thirties, forties, fifties and beyond!

Nearly 50 and still getting ID'd

47 terrific top tips by

Tristan Lee

Published by Ginger Unicorn Publishing

A CIP catalogue record for this book is available from the British Library Print Book: ISBN 978-1-910138-47-2

ISBN from our associates at Noah's House Publishing.

Ginger Unicorn Publishing
All enquiries to publishing@tristanlee.com

Editorial advice from Josie Ferguson

Cover design by Dan Debnam
Images designed by Josh Hollands
Typesetting by Lyubomyr Iatsyk
Photographs by David Long

ABOUT THE AUTHOR

Tristan Lee, aka The Gorgeousness Coach, has a zest for life and a determination to age with attitude. He is followed worldwide on social media by people eager to learn how to look good and feel great both inside and out, and how to age gorgeously. He gives a mixture of hope and belief, as well as techniques and ideas on how to make the best of yourself, wherever you are starting from.

He is now 47 years old, yet he still gets asked for ID when he buys alcohol (go to www.tristanlee.com/ID). People rarely believe him when he says how old he is each birthday (go to www.tristanlee.com/birthday). He is very much 'walking the walk'.

Tristan's passionate message is that your best years are still ahead of you, that you still matter as you get older and that it doesn't have to be downhill once you hit your 30s and beyond.

To see more of Tristan and get his regular newsletter go to tristanlee.com and to follow him on social media, you'll find him @realtristanlee on all the major platforms.

WHY 'THE GORGEOUSNESS COACH'?

People often ask me why I've called myself 'The Gorgeousness Coach'. The main reason is that a health, nutrition, wellness and self-esteem coach sounds a bit wordy and not fun or aspirational enough for me. Everywhere you look, there are people telling you to lose weight, to exercise more, eat this, don't eat that. Is it just me or can it feel a bit serious and overwhelming at times?

Whenever I tell people that I'm a Gorgeousness Coach they often smile and ask, "What does that involve?"

So, here's my reply: "I help people to look and feel gorgeous inside and out."

Making changes to our emotional and physical well-being can often appear like hard work and not much fun and that can be a real turn-off. I believe true gorgeousness is so much more than how we look. For me, it's to do with our self-worth. These days, more than ever, a lot of people's self-worth is tied up in how they look.

As 'The Gorgeousness Coach' I love to support people

make those breakthroughs, with a holistic approach which includes all aspects of self-care both internally as well as externally, helping them look and feel amazing.

ACKNOWLEDGEMENTS

This book has been a team effort and I want to show my enormous gratitude for Wes, Dan and Josh for all their incredible help. Thank you! I couldn't have done it without you guys.

Amanda for her encouragement, Claudia for her wonderful input, my gorgeous mum and family for supporting me, Katherine for giving me permission to dream, Laurence for his enthusiasm, my one-to-one coaching clients and everyone who supports what I do on social media.

Most of all I want to thank my best friend, mentor and inspiration Wes for believing in me and giving me the keys to unlock my potential so I can help others to unlock theirs.

TABLE OF CONTENTS

INTRODUCTION

Do you want to look and feel amazing in your 30s, 40s, 50s and beyond?

This book is a fun, straightforward guide to exploring how to minimise some of the physical and emotional challenges sometimes associated with getting older. I'll share with you my top tips on how to thrive as you age.

Mid-life is often the time when people re-evaluate their lives. I believe that this presents an ideal opportunity to make some small changes to improve both our physical and emotional well-being for long-term vitality and a zest for life.

In this book, I'll give you some proactive, practical hints based on many years of helping people look and feel their best as well as my own personal experience as a 47-year-old. Hence 47 tips – see what I did there?!

We are all living longer so taking care of ourselves will provide us with the health to make our olden years golden years.

In a play, all the juicy stuff usually happens in the 'second act'. The aim of this book is to empower us all to make better choices in order to run for the finish line rather than limp towards it.

Changes made earlier in life can significantly reduce many problems so often associated with ageing. For example, regular exercise and maintaining a nutritious diet can really help to sustain physical and mental health.

We will focus on small adjustments to our health, fitness and how we deal with feelings as my hope is to offer the perspective that ageing can be a time for reflection and reassessment rather than a crisis. If we view this process as an opportunity for personal growth, the experience can be greatly beneficial and rewarding. Adding some humour will hopefully make the journey fun too.

Here's to your best days still being ahead of you!

Tristan Lee

CHAPTER ONE

CATEGORY: FOOD

Tip #1
On a New-trition Mission

I believe that the key to looking and feeling good as we age is understanding that true gorgeousness is also an inside job. It surprises me that some people are very particular about their skincare and yet eat terribly. You are what you eat and poor intake will catch up with you and will ultimately result in poor output. What you allow in your mouth will show up on the outside. So, drinking plenty of water (at least 2 litres per day – which is about eight glasses) and eating a healthy diet will do wonders for your appearance.

All the moisturiser in the world counts for nothing if you're constantly shovelling junk food in your mouth. Poor quality foods including sugar-laden, fat-drenched and salt-rich products age the skin prematurely. Fresh fruits and vegetables, as well as other foodstuffs that are high in antioxidants such as blackberries, pecan nuts, dark chocolate, goji berries and blueberries, have been proven to slow down the ageing process.[1] You wouldn't put sand and mud in your car so don't put bad food in your own tank. It goes without saying that excessive alcohol consumption and smoking both dramatically accelerate the ageing process.[2]

Eating incredible, tasty food is not only great for your overall health and well-being but it will also do wonders for your looks and your mood. There are multiple reasons to prioritise what you feed yourself. We all know we should eat better, but sometimes it can be daunting to radically change what we eat – I know this myself, as I didn't always eat as well as I do now. It's only been the past few years that I've really embraced prioritising my nutrition. By embracing the five foods listed below, not only has my physique improved dramatically but my skin has also never been as clear, my energy levels have gone through the roof, I sleep better and my libido is at an all-time high!

Here's a list of my top five favourite must-have

---

[1] Schagen, S. K., Zampeli, V. A., Makrantonaki, E. and Zouboulis, C. C. (2012). *Discovering the link between nutrition and skin aging*. Retrieved from https://www.ncbi.nlm.nih.gov/pmc/articles/PMC3583891/

[2] BMJ. (2017). *Heavy drinking, smoking linked to visible signs of aging*. Retrieved from https://www.sciencedaily.com/releases/2017/11/171115195303.htm. Almasy, S. (2013). *Twins study shows smoking ages your face faster*. Retrieved from https://edition.cnn.com/2013/10/31/health/smoking-aging-identical-twins/index.html?no-st=1533467198

foodstuffs that you should include in your diet for optimum vitality and maximum gorgeousness:

1. **Quinoa**: Pronounced 'keen-wah', quinoa is high in protein and is wheat-free. There are two types – white and red – and it's a great alternative to rice, bulgur wheat and couscous. It has twice as much protein as rice and is a great source of calcium and magnesium as well as vitamins E and B. Once cooked, quinoa seeds expand to become fluffy in appearance and have anti-inflammatory properties as well as being high in dietary fibre. It's always best to rinse quinoa prior to boiling and it takes about the same time as rice to cook. I use quinoa instead of rice or couscous and I often add it to soups and sprinkle it on salads. It is available in health food stores and larger supermarkets and can be stored in an airtight container.

2. **Chia seeds:** What chia seeds lack in size they more than make up for in punch. They are jammed-full with a long list of nutrients such as protein, vitamins, Omega-3 fatty acids, fibre, iron, calcium and magnesium. Chia seeds are the Mohammed Ali of seeds. Magnesium and calcium are great for teeth and bones, Omega-3 helps to keep your heart healthy and fibre helps to maintain blood sugar and lowers cholesterol. I add them to porridge, salads and soups. They are available from health food stores and online.

3. **Coconut oil:** Now this is what you call a superfood. There are so many health benefits of coconut oil, it's hard to know where to start. It contains lauric acid which maintains cholesterol, boosts your immune system, aids digestion and helps with high blood pressure and diabetes. It's also amazing for your skin, teeth, bones and hair. I use it instead of butter on toast, cook with it rather than using olive oil and add it to soups, porridge and smoothies. Go get some, it's amazing! It's available in health shops and larger supermarkets.

4. **Sprouts (sunflower seeds, lentils, mung beans):** It is so important to eat raw, live food as sometimes the cooking process can destroy the majority of the nutrients contained within a foodstuff. Sprouted seeds are packed with anti-oxidants, vitamin E (great for skin)[3], vitamin B (which relieves stress)[4], zinc (which balances hormones, and listen up, guys

---

[3] Keen, A. M., Hassan, I. (2016). *Vitamin E in dermatology*. Retrieved from https://www.ncbi.nlm.nih.gov/pmc/articles/PMC4976416/

Michels, A. J. (2012) *Vitamin E and Skin Health*. Retrieved from https://lpi.oregonstate.edu/mic/health-disease/skin-health/vitamin-E

[4] Stough, C., Simpson, T., Lomas, J., McPhee, G., Billings, C., Myers, S., Oliver, C. and Downey, L. A. (2014). *Reducing occupational stress with a B-vitamin focused intervention: a randomized clinical trial: study protocol*. Retrieved from https://www.ncbi.nlm.nih.gov/pmc/articles/PMC4290459/

— it's essential for the development of sperm)[5]. I add them to stir-fries and sprinkle them in salads, casseroles, soups and smoothies. They are really affordable and are often available in larger health food shops. Or, why not sprout your own?

5. **Kale:** Unless you have lived in a cave, you probably know that eating greens is good for you but kale is the daddy of them all. It is one of the most nutritious plants on the planet. Curly kale is the most common variety and contains a wide assortment of vitamins (A, K, C and B6) and minerals (manganese, calcium, copper and potassium). It is also very high in anti-oxidants which helps to slow down the ageing process. A cup of kale has more vitamin C than a whole orange and it has been linked to weight-loss.[6] I chop it up small and use it raw in salads, stir-fries and smoothies. If you want to dramatically increase your nutrient intake, then kale is the way forward. It's available in larger supermarkets.

For all my latest and favourite recommendations on where to buy these and other healthy products, go to

---

[5] Freake, H. C., Govoni, K. E., Guda, K., Huang, C., Zinn, S. A. (2011) *Actions and Interactions of Thyroid Hormone Zinc Status in Growing Rats.* Retrieved from https://academic.oup.com/jn/article/131/4/1135/4686944

[6] Szalay, J. (2015). *Kale: Health Benefits & Nutrition Facts.* Retrieved from https://www.livescience.com/50818-kale-nutrition.html

www.tristanlee.com/stuff. This page is regularly updated when I find great, new stuff, so be sure to bookmark the link.

Conclusion

Making small changes is not only easy and maintainable but it will also, over time, make a big difference to your health. It will impact your grocery shopping choices as well as your cooking habits. When considering these five must-have foods, my advice is to substitute everyday foods for these healthier alternatives. This is a realistic approach to gradually making little improvements so that it doesn't feel like such a shock to your system. Bon appétit!

Tip #2
A Meaty Topic

There has been an enormous increase in vegetarianism and veganism over the past few years and I'm often asked for my advice on this topic. The numbers speak for themselves. According to *The Independent* there were 550,000 vegans in the UK in 2016 and 3.5 million in 2018, which means 7% of the UK population now identify as vegan by following a plant-based diet.[7] Personally, I gave up eating all animal products in 2015 and have never felt better. I now eat so much healthier, I prioritise good quality, nutrient-dense food more than ever and take enormous pride in what I put in my body. So, is this something you should try?

For me, the transition to a meat- and dairy-free diet was a very gradual process over many years. For some people, jumping right in may be best but I would suggest that most people make changes little by little. Why not try making a vegan dinner once a week at home? Or next time you're out at a restaurant, choose

---

[7] Petter, O. (2018). *Number of Vegans in UK Soars to 3.5 Million, Survey Finds.* Retrieved from https://www.independent.co.uk/life-style/food-and-drink/vegans-uk-rise-popularity-plant-based-diets-veganism-figures-survey-compare-the-market-a8286471.html

the vegetarian option. From there, you could expand this to two or three days a week and see how you feel. There are so many amazing, delicious, filling, quick and affordable recipes out there these days, you'll be spoilt for choice. In fact, I have a cookbook of my own coming out in the not-too-distant future, so, watch this space.

However, as far as we have come, vegetarians and vegans still sometimes get a hard time. On the other side of the coin, it is very tempting when you are passionate about something to jump up and down and tell others that they should be doing the same thing too. I've adjusted my approach; however, there are many well-meaning vegetarians/vegans who can sometimes put people off.

I truly believe in the benefits of eating less meat for a variety of reasons. Both for health as well as environmental factors, I do think the world would be a better place if we ate a more plant-based diet. However, my strategy of sharing my passion for this way of life focuses on cooking wonderful, colourful, filling and nutrient-packed meals for friends and family to show them how incredible this kind of food can taste. All made with a big dollop of T.L.C. (Tristan Loving Care!). Actions will always speak louder than words. I now have many friends who are big meat eaters asking me for some of my vegetarian recipes which is great.

There is a view that vegetarian/vegan food is dull, bland

and boring. Sadly, this can sometimes be the case and yet if done well vegetarian/vegan food can be some of the best food in the world.

Conclusion

Yes, I'd love everyone to embrace a meat- and dairy-free diet, but the way I'm going to do this isn't by condemning the food choices that others make but rather by encouraging people to consider this as an option; to be open-minded enough to explore something different: new flavours, new textures and new ingredients. It's so easy to get stuck in a food rut. When you eat less meat or dairy, it does force you to step out of your culinary comfort zone to find creative and interesting ways to fill your stomach. I now eat wonderful food every single day and I love practically helping others to do the same. If the way to a man's heart is through his stomach then eating fresh, tasty, filling plant-based food has certainly left me feeling spectacularly loved-up.

I thoroughly recommend Tasty Vegetarian and Nest & Glow cookbooks. For all my latest and favourite cookbook recommendations, go to www.tristanlee.com/stuff. This page is regularly updated when I find great, new stuff, so be sure to bookmark the link.

Please note, if you're considering going vegetarian or vegan, you need to make sure you're getting enough protein, iron and B12 from this alternative diet.

Tip #3

Want to Beat the Breakfast Blues? Top Tips for Morning Glory

I'm regularly asked about what I eat. I generally enjoy a plant-based diet (i.e. meat- and dairy-free) and I'm passionate about putting quality food into my body. Many believe that breakfast is by far the most important meal of the day. So, what do I eat on a typical morning? Here's my favourite morning routine:

The first thing I do in the morning is to drink some water. After several hours of not taking in any fluid during sleep, your body is certainly in need of hydration. If you have ever noticed that your early morning urine is darker, this is simply because of the lack of water in your system. The colour of your urine is a good indicator of your hydration levels. The clearer it is, the better. If it's the colour of Guinness then drink some water, quick!

I'm a big fan of drinking pure, clean water whenever possible. By the way, it's better for your digestive system if you sip water rather than gulp it. You should aim to drink two litres a day, which is about eight glasses. You should aim to sip it throughout the day, rather than just drinking when you're thirsty.

Next, I boil the kettle and make myself a mug of lemon in hot water. Squeeze the juice from one lemon slice (organic, unwaxed is ideal) into a cup of hot water. Leave the slice in the water and wait five minutes for it to cool a little.

Drinking lemon-infused water first thing in the morning has many incredible health benefits:[8]

1. Lemons contain potassium, calcium and magnesium which hydrate your body.
2. They're great for your joints.
3. As lemons contain citric acid they aid digestion.
4. They cleanse the liver by stimulating the release of toxins.
5. Lemons are great for sore throats as they have anti-inflammatory properties.
6. They have mood-boosting benefits as they contain potassium.
7. They clean blood vessels and arteries.
8. Lemons help to lower blood pressure.
9. They have an alkalising effect on your body and raise your PH which helps your body fight illness.

---

[8] Szalay, J. (2018). *Lemons: Health Benefits & Nutrition Facts*. Retrieved from https://www.livescience.com/54282-lemon-nutrition.html

Ware, M. (2018). *How Can Lemons Benefit Your Health?* Retrieved from https://www.medicalnewstoday.com/articles/283476.php

10. They contain vitamin C which is great for the skin.

11. They help dissolve kidney stones.

12. They relieve tooth pain.

So, what are you waiting for? Go get some lemons!

I generally wait half an hour and then toast a slice (or two) of organic rye bread and top it with coconut oil – look for extra virgin, raw, organic brands such as 'The Groovy Food Company'. I then add almond butter and slices of banana. Rye bread is a great alternative to regular bread. There are several varieties of rye bread but generally speaking, it is a dense bread so it's filling and far healthier than white bread. Look for wheat and gluten-free options, especially if standard bread tends to make your stomach bloat. Organic, raw virgin coconut oil is a wonderful alternative to butter or margarine and protein-packed almond butter is nutritionally better for you than peanut butter (which often contains sugar, salt and processed oils).

Bananas have several fantastic properties.[9] Here are just a few:

1. They increase serotonin, which boosts your mood.

---

[9] Ware, M. (2017). *Benefits and health risks of bananas*. Retrieved from https://www.medicalnewstoday.com/articles/271157.php.

2. They protect against cramps during workouts.
3. They contain large amounts of vitamin B6 which protects against diabetes, reduces inflammation and strengthens the nervous system.
4. They're low in salt and high in potassium which protects against stroke and heart attacks as well as lowering blood pressure.
5. They aid digestion.
6. They assist in the growth of healthy bacteria in the bowel.
7. They're high in fibre.
8. They're high in anti-oxidants.

Please note: If you're watching your weight, simply reduce the amount you use as these toast toppings are calorie dense.

Finally, I'm a massive porridge fan. Using a small-sized saucepan, add a small teacup of oats, a cup of water and a cup of oat or rice milk. Place on the hob and cook over a medium heat until it starts to thicken, then reduce the heat and stir regularly. Organic rolled jumbo oats are the best for texture. Add chia seeds (pumpkin, sunflower seeds are great too), a small handful of nuts (especially almond and Brazil nuts), a teaspoon of coconut oil, a splash of local honey and a sprinkling of washed blueberries. And, voila, a perfect, nutrient-packed breakfast spectacular. A healthy and filling breakfast has never tasted so good. It's like a party in your mouth!

Conclusion

So, there you have it: a window into my morning food routine. I always make time to eat a great breakfast as it really sets my energy levels up for the day ahead, especially if I'm hitting the gym. Even if you generally eat meat and dairy, try a meat/dairy-free breakfast a couple of days a week just to mix things up a little bit and break out of your food comfort zone.

Preparation is the key to success in the health department so if you don't have much time in the mornings, try overnight oats. The idea is simplicity itself: Combine oats, your choice of milk, your favourite toppings and then soak them in the fridge overnight. The oats soak up the milk, and, hey presto, your breakfast is ready and waiting for you when you wake up.

> For my favourite recipes – many of which are self-created – go to www.tristanlee.com/recipes

Tip #4

Is Your Fridge Happy or Sad? How to Avoid R.E.D. (Refrigerator Embarrassment Disorder)

I speak to so many people who tell me of their struggles to eat healthily. It seems the majority of the population experience the same challenge so fear not, it's not just you. One of the first tasks I ask new one-to-one coaching clients who are keen to make healthier food choices (that's a nice way of saying losing weight) is to go to their fridge, take a photo of the contents and send it to me*.

If your fridge is practically empty apart from a couple of mouldy onions, some out-of-date soy sauce and some margarine that Noah gave you because he didn't have room for it on The Ark, then no wonder you reach for the Chinese takeaway menu when you return home from work.

From my experience with working with loads of people who complain about eating too much junk food or that they can't be bothered to cook, more often than not it's simply a case of E.F.S. (Empty Fridge Syndrome).

So, here's a startling revelation: If you have a fridge fully stocked with delicious, healthy food you're far more likely to make better food choices than if you're staring at the insides of an empty fridge, scratching your head wondering what you're going to have for dinner.

An average fridge has four shelves, an area at the bottom for vegetables plus a couple of side shelves built into the door itself (I have a PhD in fridges). So, here's an idea of what could be on each shelf...

(I'm now going to my own fridge and this is what I actually have in there.)
N.B. I'm currently on a meat- and dairy-free diet.

Top shelf: A packet of spinach, mixed salad leaves, a packet of rocket, avocados.

Second shelf: A packet of baby tomatoes, a whole cucumber, a beetroot, spring onions, fresh coriander.

Third shelf (my pre-made shelf): A small bowl of chopped ginger in lemon juice, a small bowl of peeled garlic cloves in lemon juice, Tupperware full of boiled quinoa and sweet potato flat-bread dough.

Fourth shelf: Five whole garlic bulbs, fresh ginger, mushrooms, celery, kale, blueberries.

Bottom shelf: Six small red onions, a bag of mixed peppers, four large sweet potatoes, a bag of carrots.

Upper door shelf: A tube of tomato purée, a jar of olives, a jar of sun-dried tomatoes, a jar of organic tahini and a jar of artichokes.

Lower door shelf: Organic rice milk, coconut water, sugar-free raspberry jam, dairy-free green pesto

For food and hygiene purposes, here are some simple tips on how to organise your fridge:

Top and Middle Shelf

Ready-to-eat foods, such as dairy products, ready meals and packaged foods, leftovers, cooked meats and prepared salads. These should all be covered or kept in sealed containers to prevent contamination. Ready-to-eat foods should be stored at the top of the fridge, away from raw foods so that harmful bacteria cannot transfer from the raw food to the cooked food.

Bottom Shelf

Raw meat, poultry and fish in sealed containers to stop them touching or dripping onto other foods. Raw meats should always be stored at the bottom of your fridge to prevent cross-contamination. Ensure that each item is wrapped or in a sealed container so that they don't come into contact with other foods.

Salad Drawer

Fruit, vegetables and salad vegetables that have been washed prior to storage. Make sure that your fruit, vegetables and salad are wrapped in paper or plastic with air holes to keep them protected from any contamination. For salads and herbs, try wrapping them in a damp paper towel before storing to prevent them from drying out and to keep them fresher for longer.

Now that's a happy fridge! The next tip explains how I have a fridge of dreams so you can have one too.

> *"Men never plan to be failures; they simply fail to plan to be successful."*
>
> – William Arthur Ward

I really think there should be a very loud alarm you can buy that sounds when your fridge is less than a third full and screeches "GO SHOPPING" until you fill it with healthy food. I may invent it, what do you think?

*Fridge Photo Challenge:

So, here's a little challenge for you. Go to your refrigerator, open the door wide, step back and take a picture on your phone of what's inside your fridge. Do not remove anything. If you feel like sending me that photo, you'll find me in social media @realtristanlee. I guarantee I can tell you (without knowing anything at all about you) the current state of your health and how good your diet is.

"If you keep good food in the fridge, you will eat good food."

Now let's talk about convenience food a moment. It's really inconvenient to feel bad about yourself, your health and your weight. Convenience foods are generally full of salt, unhealthy fats and are high in calories so check labels and ingredients. Thankfully, there are some exceptions to unhealthy ready meals that are relatively healthy (EAT, Pret A Manger and Tossed have some great salad combos).

So, do yourself a massive favour and make eating healthier so much easier...go shopping! You could also consider a weekly food delivery or get into the routine that a certain day of the week is your supermarket shopping day. Make a list and you'll find you'll dramatically reduce unhealthy impulse purchases.

Top tip: Try the 'one step at a time' method in food choices – for example, start with choosing two or three of your favourite fruits and making them permanent fridge items.

Tip #5

Trick or Treat? Are Most Treats a Trick?

When I was a kid it was a real treat to have some cake, a few biscuits or some chocolate; an occasional opportunity to indulge my sweet tooth. Every Saturday morning my sister Rebecca and I would get our pocket money (about 20p – this was the 1970s) and go to our local shop to stock up on our favourite penny (and halfpenny) sweets. We would go home, watch our favourite cartoons (Scooby Doo and, of course, Tom & Jerry), scoff our faces and spend the rest of the day coming down from the sugar rush and then looking forward to repeating the same routine the following weekend.

Well, things have certainly changed. Chocolate, biscuits, cakes and a dizzying array of confectionary and snacks are now a daily (as opposed to a weekly) occurrence for most people. The word 'treat' has lost most of its meaning these days. Remember that sharp fluctuations in our blood sugar levels affect our mood. By its very definition, a 'treat' should happen occasionally in order to be fully appreciated.

As a general rule, I tend to have healthy snacks during the week and save the more indulgent treats for the weekend. Trust me, you'll enjoy it so much more if you only have cake occasionally. We often associate treats with something sweet and pleasing to look at. The good news is we can experience many of the feelings we associate with treats by simply being a little more creative in order to make healthier choices.

For example, I make my own protein balls. They're tasty, colourful and filling. To see recipes for Tristan's Tempting Treats, go to www.tristanlee.com/recipes.

Try slicing an apple and topping each slice with almond butter and some sunflower and pumpkin seeds. Or, how about plain rice cakes with peanut butter, sliced banana and pomegranate seeds? I also love to chop up fruit really small into a nice bowl and add chopped nuts, goji berries, desiccated coconut and a couple of squares of good quality dark chocolate, again chopped really small and sprinkled over the top. You get the 'feel good' factor of a treat but with far fewer empty calories (i.e. calories with little or no nutritional value) and a lot more nutrition. There's always a healthier version to your favourite go-to treat.

I believe a treat is as much about making an occasion special as it is the gastronomic experience. The English obsession with afternoon tea is a case in point. Pretty cups and saucers, matching crockery, little cakes, pastries, sandwiches and petit fours make what could be a very ordinary experience into something truly special. By taking the time to slow down and appreciate quality and attention to detail, you can experience this too.

As a huge fan of all things vintage, I absolutely love to drink my coffee out of a cup from the 1950s and even if I just slice an apple or banana and spend just a little time arranging it on a matching plate it transforms the mundane into a magical moment. We don't just eat with our mouth and stomach, we eat with our eyes too. If we invest just a couple of minutes in improving our presentation, not only will we enjoy the experience so much more but we'll probably eat less too. Also, by eating more consciously (as opposed to mindlessly demolishing a whole packet of chocolate biscuits while watching TV), we reduce the amount of food we eat.

Warning: snacking or eating treats while doing something else – being on the phone, playing computer games, catching up on the latest box-set – is a sure-fire way to eat more than you intended to.

When it comes to treats, I recommend you go for quality rather than quantity every time. Less is always more. And if you're going to have cake, have home-made cake, not the shop-bought variety. Go for colours, texture and interesting flavours for maximum appeal.

Bon appe-treat! (Alright, alright – I thought it was funny!)

Tip #6

Sugar? I'm Sweet Enough Already, Thanks...

Unless you've been living under a rock, you can't have failed to notice that sugar is the word on everyone's lips. So, it would appear that sugar is the new fat. It wasn't so long ago that fat was demonised but now sugar is enemy number one.

There are many negative consequences of consuming too much highly processed refined sugar. It has no nutritional value (as it has empty calories) and increases your risk of type 2 diabetes, weight gain, heart disease, tooth decay. So, what happens to your body when you eat sugar? Sugar consumption represses the production of leptin (which is the hormone that burns fat and lets your body know when you've had enough to eat), which can have an enormous detrimental impact on long-term good health. Therefore, reducing all types of sugar makes a HUGE difference to how you look and feel.

If you're trying to reduce your sugar intake and are reading food labels, you'll realise that sugar is hidden everywhere and this is because it's highly addictive. Food manufacturers know this so they add it to everything from pasta sauce, bread, crisps, cheese spread, tomato ketchup and even milk.

What to Do If You Have a Sweet Tooth?

The good news is that these days there are plenty of alternatives to sugar: stevia, maple syrup, agave and nectar. But a word of caution...despite the fact that these are slightly better for you, they should be used sparingly.

Warning: Artificial sweeteners should be avoided at all costs as those who "frequently consume sugar substitutes may be at an increased risk of excessive weight gain, metabolic syndrome, type 2 diabetes, and cardiovascular disease."[10]

Research also suggests that "artificial sweeteners may prevent us from associating sweetness with caloric intake. As a result, we may crave more sweets, tend to choose sweet food over nutritious food, and gain weight...(There is also) an increased risk for diabetes, cardiovascular disease and other chronic illnesses." [11] And foods labelled 'sugar-free' aren't necessarily healthier as they usually contain highly processed sweetening agents."

---

[10] Scutti, S. (2013). *4 Dangerous Effects of Artificial Sweeteners on Your Health.* Retrieved from https://www.medicaldaily.com/4-dangerous-effects-artificial-sweeteners-your-health-247543

[11] Strawbridge, H. (2012). *Artificial sweeteners: sugar-free but at what cost?* Retrieved from https://www.health.harvard.edu/blog/artificial-sweeteners-sugar-free-but-at-what-cost-201207165030

Below you can find the sugar content of well-known drinks:

McDonald's large chocolate milkshake: 13 teaspoons of sugar
Frijj chocolate drink: 12.5 teaspoons of sugar
Can of coke: 8 teaspoons of sugar
Ribena: 7 teaspoons of sugar
Redbull: 7 teaspoons of sugar
Innocent smoothie: 6.5 teaspoons of sugar
Volvic flavoured water: 6 teaspoons of sugar
Water: 0 (yay!)

Here's the rule of thumb that will change the way you look at sugar forever. 4 grams = approximately 1 teaspoon. You can now easily calculate the sugar content of your favourite beverages and make an informed decision. Knowledge is power.

Sugar and Ageing

The association between consuming too much sugar and premature ageing is now well-documented. [12] Sugar breaks down the collagen and elastin (the protein fibres that keep skin elastic, firm and plump in appearance) in

---

[12] Roux, A. E., Leroux, A., Alaamery, M. A., Hoffman, C. S., Chartrand, P., Ferbeyre, G., Rokeach, L. A. (2009). *Not So Sweet: Overconsumption of Sugar Linked to Aging*. Retrieved from https://www.sciencedaily.com/releases/2009/03/090305204328.htm

the skin leading to a dulling of the complexion, sagging skin and wrinkles. There is positive news though: It's never too late to start rebuilding your collagen levels.

Keep your eyes peeled for skincare products containing retinol. Retinol is one of the main forms of vitamin A. It's an essential vitamin needed for new cell growth, the health and maintenance of tissues and skin cells. Therefore, it plays an integral role in anti-aging skin care due to its anti-oxidant properties. I use a daily drink called 'Skinade' which helps to increase collagen and elastic from the inside.

Conclusion...Tristan's Top Sugar Tips

1. Read labels on packaging to check the sugar content (make sure to also avoid high fructose corn syrup).
2. Add more foodstuffs that contain high-level antioxidants to your diet such as blueberries, walnuts, red peppers and cranberries which will help to satisfy your sweet tooth.
3. Gradually cut down on refined sugar and reduce fizzy drinks and fruit juice. The good news is that there are so many amazing, tasty, quick and healthy ways of making your own sugar-free snacks that you can still get a sweet fix and a guilt-free treat. There's now no need to feel deprived.
4. Don't have refined sugar in the house.

5. Keep cakes, white bread and biscuits to an absolute minimum.
6. Try dark chocolate instead of milk chocolate. I love Green & Blacks 70% dark chocolate.
7. Eat more fruit. Fruit still contains natural sugar (fructose) but also fibre which helps to lessen its negative effect on blood sugar.

For my favourite recipes – many of which are self-created, go to www.tristanlee.com/recipes

Tip #7
H2-Oh I Need to Drink More Water

Did you know that a human being can survive over 21 days without food but only 3-4 days without water, whereas a camel can last up to six months without water?

Of all the things that we can do to maintain optimum health and vitality, drinking enough water is the most important. Okay, be honest, how much do you actually consume in a typical day? Don't feel bad if you only drink about four thimbles-worth, the vast majority of people are dehydrated. By the way, sorry, but caffeinated tea and coffee do NOT count as water intake because they're dehydrating.

We are about 60% water and our bodies need sufficient good quality water in order to function effectively so it makes sense to make sure we're getting plenty. We are losing water all the time (sweating, exhaling and visiting the bathroom) so we need to top up regularly.

Apart from increased energy levels and productivity, here are some more benefits of drinking water:

Promotes healthy skin
Allows cells to grow and reproduce
Boosts immune system
Flushes body waste and toxins

Lubricates joints
Regulates body temperature
Aids digestion and constipation
Relieves fatigue
Improves mood
Helps with headaches and migraines
Encourages weight-loss
Improves brain function
Fights bad breath

It can be very confusing to decide how much and what sort of water to drink. As a general rule, eight 8-ounce glasses (that's 2 litres or half a gallon) minimum should do the trick. Drink more if it's hot or you are exercising.

I have tried many different types of water from filter to bottled but currently I use a distiller water machine which heats up tap water and filters out the impurities. It tastes pure and is environmentally friendly (I stopped buying plastic bottled water a few months ago). The machine costs £130 so it's an investment but for me it's been worth every penny. See my website at www.tristanlee.com/stuff for my latest favourite healthy gadgets.

It's a highly contentious topic but I'm going to stick my neck out and declare that I'm not a fan of drinking tap water. I don't like the taste and prefer not to drink it. Do your own research and make your own decision though.

How to drink more water:

If you're not used to drinking much water, it can initially feel like you're having to force yourself to increase your intake. As with all things I would suggest that you increase the amount gradually so it's not quite such a shock to your system. Water is the essence of life and should be a pleasurable experience to imbibe. I see too many miserable-looking people trying to gulp down water like it's a punishment. If you're currently only drinking a glass a day then try 1.5 glasses and then build up to drinking more over time rather than going from one glass to eight glasses overnight. Once you understand and feel the benefits of drinking more water you'll naturally be motivated to consume more.

Sadly, alcohol dehydrates but herbal teas are fine. Green tea has been shown to increase metabolism and may aid weight loss.[13] So go pop the kettle on!

Ways to make drinking water more fun and glamorous:

1. **Make it fun:** Drink water out of a wine glass (a cocktail umbrella and a sliced strawberry on the side are an optional extra). When I distil my water, I store it in a

---

[13] Gunnars, K. (2018). *10 Proven Benefits of Green Tea.* Retrieved from https://www.healthline.com/nutrition/top-10-evidence-based-health-benefits-of-green-tea

wine bottle (I clean it out properly first). Not only is it more fun drinking water out of glass (rather than plastic), it's also better for you and it improves the taste.

2. **Add fruit:** Give your water more flavour by adding chopped up lemon, limes, blueberries or strawberries. In addition, particularly in the summer, you can make your own ice cubes.

3. **Be prepared:** I have glasses of water in most rooms: in my bathroom, on my bedside table, on my desk, in my car. And I always have a safe, portable glass bottle in my bag when I'm out and about. If it's close to hand you are so much more likely to drink it. Remember: Sip don't gulp and drink water at room temperature.

Drinking water needn't be boring or a chore. By using your imagination, it can be fun. So, get creative. I guarantee you'll feel so much better if you increase the amount of water you drink.

Eau yes you will (now that one was funny!)

Tip #8

Food, Glorious Food!

"If you fail to plan, you plan to fail."

– Benjamin Franklin

I'm curious to know: On your list of things to do each day, do you ever write the word 'eat'? Chances are the answer is a resounding NO. Pick up the dry cleaning, pay the credit card bill, mow the lawn, finish tidying the sock drawer may be on your list of tasks to do but why is it that food rarely gets a mention? You may say, "We all eat every day so we don't need to remind ourselves to do so". Yes, that's absolutely correct but would you drive for several hours on a motorway without checking if your car has petrol in it? We live in an age when 'getting things done' is the order of the day but what drives productivity? Answer: what you eat.

I find many of my new one-to-one clients often have a 'grab and go' mentality when it comes to their food choices. They'll simply pick up something when they're 'out and about'. Everywhere you go there seems to be a dizzying variety of food options so there's no need to plan ahead, right? Well, I believe not all food is created equal. If you are looking to eat healthier or lose weight, thinking ahead is essential. Most people just grab anything they can get their hands on when they're hungry. I encourage my clients to not leave food to chance but rather to adopt a proactive rather than reactive approach to what they stuff their mouths with.

We all know that hunger and making healthier food choices are not particularly compatible.

It amazes me that people will think about everything they need to do in a day but completely ignore planning what they'll eat. If you want to be more productive at work, eat better. If you want more energy to deal with the kids, make healthier food choices. If you want the health and vitality to enjoy a long life, make food a priority.

There's nothing big or clever about grabbing a microwave sausage roll from a service station (filling your stomach with rubbish fuel) while you pay for quality fuel for your car. Don't you deserve to treat your body with more respect than your vehicle?

You know at some point during the day you'll be hungry so think ahead about what you can eat.

Here are some ideas:

1. Keep healthy snacks at work and carry them around with you. Nuts (almonds, Brazils, cashews, hazelnuts), fresh fruit, seeds, celery, carrots and hummus, nut butter with banana, home-made bruffins*, home-made protein balls*, oatcakes/rice-cakes with toppings.

2. Research what the healthiest options are food-wise when you're going to a different country for the first time or on holiday.

3. Make your own lunch. You'll save an absolute fortune – probably £3-5 a day and with 200 working days a year this adds up to some serious cash.

4. Make more than you need for dinner and take the leftovers to work the following day.

5. Avoid getting so hungry that you make poor food choices. We naturally crave sugar-laden and high-fat foods when we are ravenous.

6. Be prepared to stand up for what you want. If your work colleagues or your friends all want to go to Burger King for lunch, don't give in to peer group

pressure or the need to fit in. Go to M&S, Pret or Tossed (or a local independent cafe) and grab a healthy, delicious salad.

7. When you eat food that you need to chew a lot (raw fruit and veg), you'll eat less and not feel hungry afterwards which means you're less likely to overeat.

*For these, and other, self-created recipes go to www.tristanlee.com/recipes

If you overlook food, then your health goals will be so much harder to achieve as the food we eat determines the amount of energy we have. If losing weight, feeling great and eating better is important to you then make your food choices a priority. Trust me, it is the difference between success and failure.

When I work with clients, one of the first things I ask them to do is to make a list of the food they eat for a few days so that they can become aware of what they're actually eating.

Tristan's Food Diary Challenge:

Get a diary (or do it on your phone/tablet) and for a whole week (i.e. Monday until the following Monday), write down exactly what you eat and drink at the end of each day in as much detail as possible (portion size and quantities). Be honest! This isn't about being 'good', it's simply an exercise in becoming more conscious of your eating and drinking habits in order to get a better understating of what's working (well done, keep doing it) and what isn't (let's make some changes). The key to this challenge is not to judge yourself. Instead, be curious. I have done this exercise and it can be very revealing as well as surprising. How much water did I actually drink each day? Did I really eat that many biscuits and so little fruit? When we have more knowledge, we are far better equipped to make adjustments to our food and water intake where necessary.

So, are you up for Tristan's Food Diary Challenge?

Tip #9
Say Less to Processed (Food)

These days it seems everywhere you turn, from social media, magazines and TV programmes, there doesn't seem to be a day that goes by when a new food scare doesn't hit the headlines. From concerns about bacon, eggs, sausages, milk, meat and even hobnob biscuits (not really), it seems almost everything we eat has the potential to do us enormous harm. Often, all this information that bombards us can leave us feeling confused, frustrated and, at times, mad. Or, is it just me?

How can we make healthier food choices without all this doom and gloom? Well here's my advice: As a general rule, the fewer ingredients the food you buy has, the better it is for you.

Let me tell you a story to illustrate this point. Are you sitting comfortably? Great, then let's begin...

About six years ago an incident happened whilst I was flying home to London from visiting friends in Los Angeles. I was served the in-flight breakfast which consisted of a white, cheese-filled bread roll, a blueberry muffin and a coffee. I was exceptionally hungry; however, just before tearing into it, I happened to glance at the writing on the back of the packet. I could not believe my eyes when I noticed the unbelievably long list of ingredients. It was like reading 'War and Peace'. I just could not understand how a bread roll could have 17 ingredients and a blueberry muffin 25 (with fresh blueberries nowhere to be seen). As ravenous as I was, I refused to eat either of these 'foods' and decided I would be better off eating the packaging instead, which I concluded would probably have more nutritional value.

It concerns me deeply that certain foods are so highly processed that they are able to last for years without decomposing. Shouldn't a blueberry muffin have about four ingredients in it? Flour, sugar, eggs and blueberries?

So, here's my rule of thumb: When buying food, go for choices that are as natural as possible, which haven't been pumped full of chemicals, preservatives and additives. Start looking at the list of ingredients on packaging. If it's longer than a paragraph, don't buy it.

Real food = few preservatives and additives.

Remember that ready meals are usually high in salt, sugar and fat. They're also packed with empty calories and often not very filling so you end up eating a lot more than you need to.

Conclusion:

If you're going to eat cake or biscuits at least eat those that are home-made. These days there are so many amazing, healthy, delicious, cheap and quick recipes that you can make yourself if you need a sweet treat just by throwing 3-4 ingredients together. So rather than eating rubbish 'food', let me show you a couple of my own recipes that taste incredible, are ridiculously easy to make and will also save you loads of money.

BONUS!

Here's a couple of my favourite, most gorgeous, self-created snacking recipes:

Tristan's Gorgeous Protein Balls

Time: *5 mins*
Cost: about 50 pence for 6-8 balls

Half a cup of coconut water (or plain water)
2 heaped teaspoons of almond or peanut butter
Zest of 1 lemon (grated)
½ teaspoon cinnamon
Juice of half a lemon
1 teaspoon chia seeds
1-2 teaspoons maple syrup (depending on how sweet you want them)
1 cup fine oats
Desiccated coconut (for dusting)
Pomegranate seeds (optional)

Melt the coconut water and nut butter together over a medium heat and blend together until smooth using a wooden spook, then turn the heat off. Once the mixture has blended smoothly together turn the heat off and add the lemon zest, cinnamon, lemon juice, chia seeds, maple syrup and oats. Blend all the ingredients thoroughly together.

Dust a chopping board with the desiccated coconut and

using a tablespoon or teaspoon scoop out the mixture onto the coconut then roll into balls.

Stick in the fridge to chill for 10 mins and put the kettle on.

Optional extra: Using a thimble or the end of a wooden spoon, make a dent in the top and add pomegranate seeds.

Double or triple the quantities for a bigger batch.

Tristan's Tempting Sweet Potato Flatbread

1 teaspoon salt (I use pink Himalayan)
½ teaspoon chilli powder
2½ teaspoons mixed herbs
½ teaspoon cayenne pepper
1 teaspoon sunflower seeds
1 teaspoon pumpkin seeds
2 cups flour (I use spelt flour)
2 cups cooked, mashed sweet potatoes (peeled)
Freshly ground black pepper
1 teaspoon coconut oil

Preheat the oven to 180 degrees.

Put all the herbs, seeds and spices into a mixing bowl. Sieve in the flour and blend together.

Add the mashed sweet potatoes to the flour and herbs and knead together until all the flour is completely absorbed. If the mixture seems wet and sticky then add a couple more tablespoons of flour (some sweet potatoes have more moisture and will require a bit more flour). Allow the dough to rest for 5-10 minutes.

Dust a chopping board with flour then take a quarter of the dough and shape into a ball. Use a rolling pin and roll out one quarter of an inch thick. Use more flour to avoid sticking.

Add a level teaspoon of coconut oil into a baking tray and melt in the oven for a couple of minutes. Add the sweet potato flatbread and pop into the oven for approx. 12 minutes (flip halfway through). Check with a fork to see if it's cooked. (If it's still soft and soggy it's not ready but if it's firm then it is.)

Cover the remaining dough with a damp tea towel to keep the bread from drying out. The dough lasts up to five days in the fridge. Double up the ingredients to make a bigger 'family size' batch.

For my favourite recipes – many of which are self-created – go to www.tristanlee.com/recipes

CHAPTER TWO

CATEGORY: FITNESS

Tip #10
Slow and Steady Wins the Race

When it comes to fitness, one of my absolute top tips is to pace yourself. When I work with my one-to-one clients who want to get fitter, I always tell them not to jump straight into the deep end. It's so tempting when we want to make changes to our levels of physical activity to feel that we have to go totally crazy and go to the gym six times a week. January 1st is a prime example of this. Fitness centres are jam-packed full of people desperate to shed months of over-eating in just a couple of weeks. When the weight fails to drop off immediately, they often quit. Going hell for leather is simply not sustainable. People also ramp up their fitness activity too quickly. It's much better to gradually increase the frequency and intensity over several months rather than doubling how much cardio you do or how much you lift every week.

It's human nature to want to see results quickly but it rarely works. New year motivation and resolutions are great but they only get you so far. In my experience, it's much more effective to ease your way into increasing the amount of exercise you do in sync with the seasons. During winter our bodies are designed to conserve energy so work with your biology and gear up your exercise towards spring and summer. Don't give yourself a hard time.

So, how could that look in reality?

January, Feb and March: two workouts a week
April, May and June: three workouts a week
July and August: four workouts a week

This is much better than:

January 1st to January 14th: six workouts a week
January 14th to end of January: three workouts a week
February: two workouts a week
March: one workout a week
April: Quit!

Ease yourself into a new fitness routine so as to not shock your body. Fitness needs to build up gradually. When I started weight-training my personal trainer said you can't rush the process and that it would take three to five years of consistent effort to reach and maintain my physique and fitness. In my case, he was right. By setting realistic and long-term expectations we are so much more likely to succeed. For some people, this may be quicker than for others depending on their goals and where they're starting from.

When it becomes a habit rather than relying on motivation and will-power alone, not only are you more likely to reach your goals, you'll also enjoy the process so much more. By understanding this philosophy, you will avoid the trap of beating yourself up for not being able to maintain six workouts a week.

Slow and steady wins the race so commit to at least 6-12 months of moderate exercise instead of what most people do which is giving themselves just 2-4 weeks to get the beach body of their dreams. Relax, there's no rush. I start making tiny fitness increases and improvements in January and then very, very slowly built up to achieving my summer holiday beach goals. It may not sound very glamorous compared to the headline-grabbing promises of 'drop a dress size in 12 minutes' or 'lose a stone by Friday' but this approach works. Remember the story of the tortoise and the hare? I have many friends (hares) that raced ahead of me with their fitness progress as I plodded along (tortoise) but many fell by the wayside unable to maintain that level of intensity. I eventually won the race and you can too.

Alternative Exercises to Going to the Gym

If you hate the idea of the gym or think you don't have time to exercise, here are some simple ways of getting exercise into your daily routine:

1. Get off the bus a couple of stops sooner and walk the

rest of the way.

2. Take the stairs instead of the lift.
3. Speed-walk whilst doing errands.
4. Play in the park.
5. Go the long route to your destination.
6. Add 15 minutes to your dog walking time.
7. Clean your own car.

Tip #11
Want to Be a Fitness Stud? Get an Exercise Bud

In my experience of working one-to-one with people over the years, a great many seem to struggle to get a handle on getting fit. So many of us start with great intentions and yet fail to stay at it long enough to enjoy the results we seek. Why is this? There are many reasons for this from unrealistic expectations and lack of focus to no clear goal and wanting results too quickly.

I'd like to add to this list, if I may?

For me, there is a vital missing ingredient in order to achieve long-term physical fitness: support, encouragement and accountability which all fall under the banner of 'teamwork'.

I remember attending a health and wellness seminar many years ago. The main thing I took away from this event (apart from various goodie bags and free samples) was the idea that most people fail to maintain food and fitness habits due to trying to 'go it alone'. What I concluded from this event was...Don't be a lone ranger.

There's really no need to go it alone and do it all by yourself. It can be a lonely and sometimes overwhelming experience to start a fitness and food journey especially if you feel that you have a big mountain to climb.

From working with clients for many years, I have learnt that every single person needs a bit (or a lot) of praise, encouragement and support. It's really hard for a single lump of coal to stay lit but surround that coal with other like-minded lumps of coal and together they will keep the flame burning bright. So, seek out other people to help keep you on track and make the process more fun.

Habits and routine make keeping on track so much easier.

So, what could that actually look like in reality? Here are some ideas:

1. Find a friend or work colleague who wants to be your fitness buddy. Someone who you can exercise with. Whether it's running twice a week, going to a spin class, walking or playing squash finding fun, creative ways to work together is extremely beneficial.

2. It really helps if you can fit exercise around your current routine: going to the gym together after work on a Tuesday and Thursday or inviting a fellow mum (or dad) to accompany you for a 30-minute walk before collecting the children from school three times a week.

3. Ideally find 2-3 fitness buddies so if one is busy,

unwell, unmotivated or has disappeared into a witness protection scheme then you'll still have someone to work out with.

4. By scheduling an 'exercise appointment' with another person, you're far more likely to do it. If it's a loose intention, chances are it simply won't happen. So, put it in your diary and make it a priority rather than an afterthought.
5. If you are unable to find a fitness buddy, or just prefer to exercise alone, then why not ask a friend or family member if you can be accountable to them? Start the week by sending them a text outlining your exercise plan for the week ahead and check in with them each time you've achieved your goal. Accountability is such an incredible way of moving your fitness aspirations from a vague desire into concrete action.

At the end of the day, this is really all about feeling good about yourself and taking action no matter how small. We all know how procrastination can really weigh us down but by learning simple, fun ways to encourage activity you'll not only feel lighter and more energised but your self-esteem will also dramatically improve.

Focus on small steps and the activity and the results will follow. Don't keep your fitness challenges to yourself. Being a secret agent may work for James Bond but it's not the ideal scenario to achieve, keep and ultimately enjoy an ongoing relationship (as opposed to a one night stand) with physical activity.

In conclusion, one of the keys to improving your levels of fitness is to find fun fitness activities and where possible, do them with a friend. Friends can encourage you when you're feeling unmotivated and vice versa. And, remember, the most important reason to get fitter is the incredible impact it can have on your self-worth and confidence. Nothing looks as good as fitness feels.

Here are a few fitness goals you could have:

Run a 5k race.
Play in a sports match.
Jog for 15 minutes without stopping.
Walk up the three flights of stairs to your office each day rather than take the lift/elevator.
Do ten press-ups in a row.

> Remember: Exercise is not just about losing weight, it can also be about lowering cholesterol or high blood pressure, reducing stress and raising self-esteem.

Tip #12
The Power of Association

"You are the result of the five people you spend the most time with." – Jim Rohn

Birds of a feather flock together, so who are you hanging around with? Human beings are social animals. We create communities, tribes and connections that can have both positive and negative consequences. Yet, most of us never consider the impact on us of who we spend time with.

What's the current state of your health, fitness, finances, level of positivity? Chances are if you're making unwise food choices, the people you spend the most time with also do the same. If you hang around with four unfit people, chances are you will be number five. If you feel negative about yourself or life in general, there's a really good chance your nearest and dearest feel the same way.

It's really hard to make changes or maintain good habits if your environment doesn't support you. It's a fact that we human beings like to build relationships with people like ourselves. We like to fit in, to belong and spend time in familiar social groups. We all need and enjoy the stability that being part of a tribe brings (friends and work colleagues, for example), but the saying 'familiarity breeds contempt' is also very true.

Perhaps it's time to take a step back and ask yourself if those around you are inspiring you or not? I know this can sound harsh but understanding this concept is essential if you want to thrive both physically and emotionally. Making changes is so much easier if others around you are doing the same. If your partner, children, workmates have positive habits, chances are you will too. It's a bit like osmosis, whether we like it or not we simply cannot escape the influence of those around us.

So how does this look in reality? Why do we still spend time with friends and family even if they aren't having the best influence on our health and fitness goals? People fall into three categories:

1. One hour.
2. One day.
3. One week.

Some people are best to spend just an hour with, others a whole day and the last group for an entire week. So, what does this actually mean? Choose who you spend time with the most very carefully and limit the amount of time if necessary.

If everyone you know is overweight, seek out the company of people who aren't. If your nearest and dearest don't exercise, look around for someone who is in great shape and befriend them. If all your work colleagues whinge and moan about life every Friday night at the pub, maybe find other people who have a positive, can-do attitude to socialise with more.

Here's an example of how to make contact with people you want to spend more time with whether it is on the phone, at the gym, in a coffee shop, at the school gates or in an art class.

"Hi, I've noticed you're in great shape/eat really healthily/always so optimistic etc., I'd absolutely love to buy you to a quick coffee sometime soon to find out more about how you keep so fit/what you eat/what makes you so happy. Would that be okay?"

I guarantee people will be flattered by this approach. People love to be complimented and talk about themselves. Who knows, you may learn something new and even make new friends. Why not give it a go? Stepping out of your social comfort zone can make the difference between success and failure.

> *"If you always do what you've always done, you'll always get what you've always got."*
>
> – Henry Ford

Have You Ever Heard the Story of the Crabs in a Bucket?

There once was a man walking along the beach and he saw another man fishing. As he got closer he saw the man had a bucket with no lid and inside there were live crabs.

"Why don't you cover your bucket so the crabs won't escape?" he asked.

"You don't understand", the other man replied. "If there was one crab in the bucket it would surely crawl out very quickly. However, when there are many crabs in the bucket, if one tries to crawl up the side, the others grab hold of it and pull it back down so that it will share the same fate as the rest of them."

It's the same with people. Sometimes when we try to do something different or improve our fitness and lifestyle, others may try to drag us back down as it can be very unsettling and threatening when someone 'breaks rank'. So, ignore the other crabs. Charge ahead and do what is right for you. It may not be easy and you may not succeed as much as you'd like, but you will NEVER share the same fate as those who never try.

So, choose to 'climb the crab bucket' instead of listening to others.

Tip #13
Are You Sleeping Beauty?

Do you get a good night's sleep? Do you sleep like a baby or is your slumber broken and of poor quality? Few things affect your overall health and appearance more than a restful and peaceful night's sleep. How many hours do you get on average? When you wake, do you feel refreshed or stressed?

Sleep is incredibly important yet some people don't value getting quality sleep and therefore don't prioritise it. Sleep is vital for your well-being. Our body and skin repair themselves at night and your brain needs this 'down time' to process all the events of the day. In times of war, sleep deprivation is sometimes used as a form of torture to force captives to reveal secret information. Lack of sleep can actually drive you crazy and seriously affect your immune system.[14]

Q: So, what is a good night's sleep?
A: The Five Rs. Waking up feeling rested, relaxed, restored, recharged and raring to go.

---

[14] University of Washington Health Sciences/UW Medicine. (2017). *Chronic sleep deprivation suppresses immune system: Study one of first conducted outside of sleep lab*. Retrieved from www.sciencedaily.com/releases/2017/01/170127113010.htm

If this isn't your current sleep experience then some adjustments are necessary.

Bedtime Routine

A lot of people I've spoken to feel sleep-deprived or have difficulty getting a good night's sleep. So, here's the question: Do you get 'ready' for bed or do you 'stumble' into bed after falling asleep on the sofa? The key is 'preparing' for bed. What do you do before bedtime?

Watching TV is most people's way of unwinding in the evening but depending on what you watch it can be anything but relaxing. If the last thing you see before going to bed is depressing news, a violent film, a disturbing documentary, a stressful sports match or arguments on a soap opera or reality TV show, then no wonder you don't sleep well. During sleep, your mind 'digests' what it has absorbed during the day so be aware and vigilant what you 'feed' it.

My night-time routine sets me up for a good night's sleep, does yours?

Your skin repairs itself at night so give it a helping hand. Going to bed with clean skin not only feels great but it's also a fantastic way of relieving stress. If dirt, grease or pollution is left on the surface of your skin overnight it's a recipe for blocked pores, blackheads and whiteheads. Getting into this habit is essential for great skin. So, wash your skin ***before*** you get too tired.

Here's an example of a great night-time routine:

Get ready for bed before you're really tired e.g. after you've watched the nightly news and before you make your evening cup of cocoa.

Wash your face, brush your teeth, floss and moisturise. Read something inspiring or interesting for a few minutes in bed.

Why not write down three things you've achieved during the day. This helps to focus the mind on what you've accomplished during that day rather than what you haven't. For example: went for a run, had a healthy lunch, called a client about a meeting. It is so easy to dwell on what you've not achieved. This activity is great for your mental health and helps to celebrate your successes.

So, what have you done today that you can be proud of? No matter how small, write it down. It's also a nice habit to write down three things that you're grateful for.

Diet

What do you eat or drink before bed? Cheese, meat, dairy, alcohol and caffeinated drinks (coffee, tea, energy drinks, soft drinks) will all affect how you sleep. Also, how soon before going to bed do you eat/drink them? If your metabolism is overloaded with foods and beverages that are challenging to digest then your body will not be able to relax as effectively. Therefore, don't eat a heavy meal before bedtime and make it a habit to drink herbal tea after your evening meal, such as chamomile tea, which has a calming effect[15] or peppermint tea which aids digestion.[16]

Tips for Gorgeous Slumber

Is your bedroom a place of calm and serenity? Your environment plays a pivotal part in encouraging a good night's sleep. If your bedroom looks more like a war zone than a sanctuary then it's time to clear the clutter and create a space that promotes rest rather than stress.

1. Tidy away clothes, pick up laundry and remove dirty mugs and plates.
2. Make sure you have a decent mattress. It's fascinating that people are happy to spend a great deal of money on a sofa or dining table but will use an old bed for decades. My particular favourites are good quality memory foam mattresses, which are amazing and support your back.
3. Invest in high-quality bed linen. Your bed should be

---

[15] Villines, Z. (2017). *What are the benefits of chamomile tea?* Retrieved from https://www.medicalnewstoday.com/articles/320031.php

[16] Ware, M. (2017). *What are the benefits of mint?* Retrieved from https://www.medicalnewstoday.com/articles/275944.php

somewhere you feel safe and comfortable in. You spend a third of your life sleeping so put your money where your body is. If you have thread-bare sheets, tatty pillowcases and old pillows then it's high time to get rid of them and get some new bedding.

4. Add a couple of drops of good quality lavender oil onto your pillow. Lavender has relaxing and calming properties.[17]

5. Buy thick curtains that block out the light as this can be very effective for creating the right atmosphere for a good night's sleep.

All these things combined help to 'invite' sleep. Sleep is like seduction. You need to take your time and gently 'woo' sleep into your bed with you.

Sweet dreams.

---

[17] Axe, J. *10 Lavender Oil Benefits for Both Major and Minor Ailments.* Retrieved from https://draxe.com/lavender-oil-benefits/

Nordqvist, J. (2018). *What are the health benefits and risk of lavender?* Retrieved from https://www.medicalnewstoday.com/articles/265922.php

Tip #14
Exercise: Variety is the Spice of Life

Evidence shows there are more gyms opening and people are increasingly spending more on their fitness.[18] That, coupled with the popularity of fitness magazines, has seen more people than ever want to get in shape. Yet, it can be challenging to get started and confusing what to do to get maximum results.

I'm a massive fan of doing a wide variety of exercise like yoga, Pilates, running, rock climbing, weight-training or Zumba in order to get healthy, improve fitness and generally feel fantastic.

Not only will exercise improve the shape of your body but it will also do wonders for your self-esteem. Even moderate levels of exercise have been found to have a significant impact on health. Also, as our bodies age our bone density and muscle mass decrease so using weights (resistance training) can help minimise the effects of this.

---

[18] Smithers, R. (2015). *UK gym membership spending up by 44%*. Retrieved from https://www.theguardian.com/lifeandstyle/2015/aug/18/uk-gym-membership-spending-up-by-44-per-cent

Minto, D. (2017). *2017 State of the UK Industry Report – Out Today.* Retrieved from http://www.leisuredb.com/blog/2017/5/5/2017-state-of-the-uk-fitness-industry-report-out-now

Slim, fit bodies are synonymous with youth and vitality. My exercise advice is that any activity that keeps the body in shape, that encourages flexibility and increases circulation is good for you.

Add to this the statistics, reported in the World Health Organisation (WHO) 2018 Fact Sheet, that physically active adults have a 20% to 30% reduced risk of premature death compared to people who are insufficiently active and up to a 50% reduced risk of developing major chronic diseases such as coronary heart disease, stroke, diabetes and cancers. The benefits of exercising are crystal clear.

Fit as a Fiddle

There is a myth about exercise that for it to be worthwhile you have to spend hours in the gym pumping iron and making a lot of grunting noises. I disagree. We are all unique and our bodies have individual needs and capabilities. As such, there are many ways to keep active and get your heart rate up:

Jogging
Fast-paced walking
Cycling
Paddling
Rock climbing
Dancing
Sex!

Swimming
Squash
Basketball
Football
Netball
Line dancing
Hockey
Hiking
Oh, and did I mention sex?

You can really make a difference to your overall health and vitality by simply walking more and driving less. It is frightening how little we walk these days.

Is this your typical day?
Drive to work, take the lift to your floor, sit at a desk all day, drive home and sit on the sofa all evening. Repeat.

If this is you then you are what's known as 'sedentary', basically completely inactive. Sadly, you're missing out on the many phenomenal benefits of exercise.

Top Tip: Walk More! Here's How:

Walk up the stairs rather than taking the lift.
Offer to take a friend's dog for a walk.
Go to the park to walk a lap or two on the way to the pub.
Walk the long (scenic) route to the shops.
Use your lunch break for a walk rather than sitting in the canteen looking at social media.

Make it simple for yourself and find something you enjoy. We sometimes have the idea that exercise means spending 90 minutes at the gym, three times a week. This is not necessarily the case. I personally would rather go for a run outside than use a treadmill. Twenty minutes doing something that gets your heart-rate up is far better than nothing at all, and doing something you actually enjoy makes exercising fun rather than it feeling like a chore to complete as quickly as you can.

Actually, doing a little exercise and often is much better than going crazy for a few days and then stopping for six months. Consistency is the key. Once you have a routine, you have momentum and results will start to appear. It starts to become part of who you are. The effort of getting back on track if you stop is often enormous so start small and build up over time. You're setting yourself up for failure if you're planning to go to the gym four times a week or run three times a week and lose 5kg by the end of the month. Most people are impatient for dramatic results and yet the only way to achieve lasting success in any area of your life is by taking a long-term view. So, how about one hour, twice a week and after a few weeks try three times a week? Then keep increasing your exercise time gradually from there.

I used to really struggle with exercise. I would think about going for a run for such a long time that it meant I often had time to talk myself out of it. You know what I mean:

"It's too cold."
"I don't feel like it."
"It's too hot."
"There's something on TV I really can't miss."
"I'll go after I eat."
"I'll go before I eat."

I learned a very helpful lesson: just put your trainers on and leave the house. Don't dwell on those thoughts (excuses!) or you will never go.

Perhaps it comes from primitive times of not wanting to use valuable energy unless it's completely essential. The key is to start where you are. If fast walking is all you can manage, then do that and feel proud of yourself for doing something rather than beating yourself up for not running six miles.

The key is to find something you enjoy. Work with others if it spurs you on. Try a variety of different things to see what's out there. Exercise really can be an extremely fulfilling experience.

Happy exercising, guys!

Tip #15

Face Exercises: Take It on the Chin(s)

If you think that saggy skin and a droopy jawline go hand-in-hand with getting older then, breaking news: You can significantly reduce this happening by stimulating your facial muscles to keep them active.[19] If you don't 'exercise' your facial muscles they can lose their firmness and gravity will take over. The notion that all jowls are inevitable is simply a myth.

We all know that if you want to keep your body healthy and in shape then lifting weights is highly effective. The same is true for your face. Many years ago, I watched a TV programme about facial workouts (which at the time I thought was absolutely hilarious) and I have been doing them ever since. So far, no jowls! These are simple face exercises that stretch and tone your muscles to stimulate blood flow to the face. One of the main causes

[19] Macdonald, F. (2018). *Scientists are Investigating Facial Exercises to Make You Look Younger.* Retrieved from https://www.sciencealert.com/facial-yoga-can-make-you-look-younger-no-fillers-or-creams-science.

of sagging skin is simply a lack of muscle movement.[20]

And for guys who shave, the good news is that this is an ideal opportunity to kill two birds with one stone: You exercise your muscles when you twist and pull your face to get the angle right to shave. Without even realising it you are already stretching and toning those facial muscles so well done you! The key to face exercises is to slow down and exaggerate each movement so you can maximise the benefits. Ladies can also benefit too as the same principle applies when you're applying moisturiser.

Here are some exercises that can help you tone your facial muscles:

Initially, it is best to practise in the mirror. So, let's wake up those lazy face muscles.

Exercise 1: The Pout

GENTLY tilt your head back, look at the ceiling and pull your bottom lip over your top lip to feel the sensation of your neck muscles stretching. This is my favourite stretch for toning and keeping the dreaded double chin at bay. Place both hands on your collarbone to add a bit more resistance. Be careful initially not to strain your

---

[20] Northwestern University. (2018). *Facial exercises help middle-aged women appear more youthful.* Retrieved from www.sciencedaily.com/releases/2018/01/180103160142.htm

neck as this is an intense movement, so easy does it until you've got the hang of it. Gently patting your face to encourage blood flow to these muscles is also effective. Repeat five times.

Exercise 2: The Cheesy Grin

Smile showing all your teeth and imagine this smile reaching back to your ears. Do this slowly, exaggerating the movement. This is great for your cheeks and jawline. Repeat five times.

Exercise 3: The 'Squirrel'

Fill your cheeks with air like a squirrel with a mouth full of nuts, then release the air. This is amazing for your cheeks. Repeat five times.

Repeat these exercises three times a week for maximum benefit.

Conclusion

By practising face exercises, you can radically reduce the effects of gravity. Simply being aware of moving your face more often to keep those muscles awake and active will make a significant difference. We are creatures of habit and that also applies to our faces. We get used to moving or not moving our faces in certain ways. Occasionally stopping and stretching your face can keep sagging skin taut. I sometimes do this in the car and I often get funny looks from other drivers but I'll have the last laugh when I have a youthful jawline when I'm in my 80s. The sooner you start the better, but at any age you can begin to activate those dormant muscles to avoid having a face like a bulldog.

Tip #16

Are You Stretching Yourself?

Whether you currently keep fit or not, everywhere you look from magazines to television and all over social media, staying in shape has become the thing to do. And yet, rarely is the subject of stretching mentioned. Sadly, it seems completely overlooked by most people.

I studied as a dancer and staying flexible was a fundamental part of the training. Not only did it help to make me a better dancer, it also helped to prevent injuries by warming up the muscles prior to physical exertion. A top priority for dancers and athletes is to be aware of and to respect their bodies. I feel we all should have a better understanding of our physicality. When we reach mid-life and beyond, maintaining a level of suppleness is essential to providing a greater quality of life during our second half.

Maintaining mobility can be difficult as we get older. Muscles and joints weaken and our range of movement generally deteriorates with age.

There are many benefits to stretching. Here are my top three:

1. Stretching reduces lower back pain and arthritis.

Regular stretching improves flexibility. The range of

motion and the level of elasticity relieves stiffness in the afflicted joints. Understandably it may be difficult and painful to stretch or move these joints. To help reduce the pain, it's best to warm up stiff muscles prior to stretching with a heat pack and cool down muscles with an ice pack following exercise to minimise swelling. You may also want to consider assisted stretching by using stretching equipment or with the help of another person.

2. Stretching helps to improve poor posture.

As we age we lose elasticity and flexibility. So many people spend years sitting hunched over a desk and over time this will likely result in poor posture. Poor posture is defined by a forward head posture, rounded shoulders and upper back as well as forward pressing hips. The good news is that with a simple, consistent stretching routine you can improve flexibility and loosen tight ligaments, tendons and muscles to give you a greater range of motion. You can also add strength training exercises to your stretching routine; This will help balance out the weaker muscles, supporting you to correct poor posture with the benefits of flexibility.[21]

3. Stretching increases blood flow and energy levels.

---

[21] LifeSpan. (2018). *Health Benefits of Stretching for Older Adults.* Retrieved from https://www.lifespanfitness.com/uk/fitness/resources/articles/health-benefits-of-stretching-exercises-in-older-adults?   store=uk

Dynamic stretching (such as arm swings, shoulder circles, lunges, leg swings) is a low-intensity form of stretching that can incorporate movements which will stretch your muscles. This is different to static stretching, which is stretching while your body is not in motion. As well as lengthening your muscles, dynamic stretches also increase circulation and nutrient flow throughout the body which helps increase the body's energy levels.[22]

While regular stretching is a great way to help manage lower back pain, improve posture and increase energy levels, there are additional exercises that will aid healthy ageing such as Tai Chi, Pilates and Yoga.

So, make stretching part of your fitness routine. It's all too tempting to neglect but the benefits are so enormous you'd be crazy not to. Stretching affects your psychological state as well so join an exercise class, use one of the many YouTube stretching tutorials or simply ask a personal trainer at your gym to show you some stretching routines. Take it nice and easy though and build up over time to avoid strain or potential injury.[23]

---

[22] LifeSpan. (2018). *Health Benefits of Stretching for Older Adults*. Retrieved from https://www.lifespanfitness.com/uk/fitness/resources/articles/health-benefits-of-stretching-exercises-in-older-adults?   store=uk

[23] Murlasits, Z., Reed, J. Wells, K. (2012). *Effect of resistance training frequency on physiological adaptions in older adults*. Retrieved from https://www.sciencedirect.com/science/article/pii/S1728869X12000081

Tip #17

Don't Resist Resistance Training

When most people think of physical activity, usually it is aerobic training, such as walking, running, swimming or cycling that comes to mind. As much as it is true that cardiovascular training has many health benefits, there is also a great deal of evidence that strength training is incredibly useful as we age. Most people associate resistance training with increasing muscle mass but there are many more positives for incorporating this kind of exercise into our lives after 40 and beyond. An ideal exercise routine combines resistance training alongside cardiovascular activity, therefore, giving us balanced, overall results.

"Resistance training is any exercise that causes the muscles to contract against an external resistance with the expectation of increases in strength, tone, mass and/or endurance. The external resistance can be dumbbells, rubber exercise tubing, your own body weight, bricks, bottles of water or any other object that causes the muscles to contract."[24]

---

[24] Retrieved from http://speedalliancetraining.com/resistance-training-pembroke-pines-fl/

Here are my top four reasons not to resist resistance training as we get older:

1. It really helps to maintain muscle mass.

The bad news is that from the age of 25 onwards we gradually lose muscle mass particularly as we hit our late 50s. The good news is that although we cannot completely prevent this process, we can significantly reduce the rate at which we lose muscle mass in our middle years and beyond. Including resistance training in your exercise routine will really benefit your training. Also, performance is increased when your muscles are stronger.

2. You can achieve a lot in a short space of time.

By doing just 15 to 20 minutes three times a week, you can significantly increase your strength. Don't be concerned if you think you'll have to lift heavy weights because you can achieve great results simply by pushing yourself just a little more than you usually do.

3. Helps to maintain weight.

The classic equation to losing weight is to reduce your calorie intake, burn calories by keeping fit or doing both. Unfortunately, sometimes when we lose weight we can lose some muscle as well so it can be challenging to do both. Balancing any weight loss with maintaining muscle mass as we age is, therefore, a top priority.

4. You'll see a reduction in injuries.

Many of us experience joint pain as we age. Our bones and muscles work in conjunction with our joints to help move and support us. Exercise can significantly strengthen our joints from becoming sore, weak and stiff as we get older. When we have stronger joints, we have better balance and we are therefore better protected against hurting ourselves if we should ever fall. We can reduce some of the physical anxiety and vulnerability often associated with ageing by exercising. You'll find that even everyday activities such as gardening, housework and DIY can be beneficial.

Personal Trainer Gregg Harvey explains:
"Resistance training helps build muscle which helps you burn more calories. The more muscle you have the higher your metabolism. When you do cardio you are burning a decent amount of calories but when you stop and your heart rate comes down, that high-calorie burn stops. Therefore, adding resistance training to our exercise routine as we get older, is a really great idea."

There are many ways you can strengthen your muscles, whether at home or in the gym.

Different types of resistance training include:

Free weights – classic strength training tools such as dumbbells or barbells.

Weight machines – devices that have adjustable seats with handles attached either to weights or hydraulics.

Medicine balls – weighted balls.

Resistance bands – like giant rubber bands – these provide resistance when stretched. They are portable and can be adapted to most workouts. The bands provide continuous resistance throughout a movement.

Your own body weight – can be used for squats, push-ups and chin-ups.

And don't forget: Getting enough sleep and having a healthy diet is essential to getting the most out of resistance training. Both assist the body to grow and maintain muscle tissue.

CHAPTER THREE

CATEGORY: FACES

Tip #18
Sun Safety: The Sun Has Got His Hat On – Do You?

It's a fact of life that we age. Sadly, it's not something you can escape or avoid. The truth is that some people age well and some don't; however, the good news is that we can make a massive difference to how we age.

So many of the signs that we associate with ageing – for example, wrinkles and saggy skin – can be helped by taking care of ourselves. Protecting our faces with sunscreen to minimise the damaging effects of UV light has a significant impact on how we age. As a 47-year-old guy who still regularly gets asked for ID when buying alcohol (see for yourself www.tristanlee.com/ID), I know a thing or two about slowing down the ageing process and maintaining a youthful appearance for as long as possible.

Here are my top tips for minimising the ageing effects of sun exposure.

Sun Protection

Sunlight is responsible for 80% of the signs we associate with ageing[25] such as wrinkles and fine lines because it breaks down collagen and elastin which help to keep the skin looking firm. Using moisturisers containing sun protection factor (SPF) daily on your face, on the front and back of your neck and your hands is a sure-fire way of protecting those areas that are vulnerable to sun exposure. Use every day, even in winter, for maximum results.

How to Have Fun in the Sun Without Feeling the Burn

I'm sure many of us agree that a golden tan looks wonderful. People look healthier, happier, slimmer and more attractive with a suntan. And yet, the fact remains that tanned skin is damaged skin. A tan is your skin's way of protecting itself from the harmful effects of the sun.

If you have naturally pale skin, burn easily, have freckles or red hair then you'll need to be particularly careful in the sun. Yet, if you have a darker skin tone, tan easily and rarely burn then perhaps you can have a slightly more relaxed approach to sun protection due to higher

---

[25] Flament, F., Bazin, R. Laquieze, S., Rubert, V., Simonpietri, E., Piot, B. (2013). *Effect of the sun on visible clinical signs of aging in Caucasian skin.* Retrieved from https://www.ncbi.nlm.nih.gov/pmc/articles/PMC3790843/

levels of melanin in the skin. The key here is to work with your skin type.

The Sun Has Got Its Hat On – Hip, Hip, Hooray!

Sunshine lifts the mood, boosts energy levels and stimulates the production of vitamin D, which is vital for good health and well-being as well as keeping your bones and teeth healthy. As much as I am a fan of sunscreen, I also believe that constantly slapping loads of chemical-laden lotion on our body is not ideal either because many brands contain harsh chemicals which aren't ideal for your health; therefore, use with caution. If in doubt, stay in the shade!

Vitamin D-lightful

Your body needs sun exposure, but just not in excess. 15-30 minutes of direct sunlight per day, on as much of your body as you dare to bare, has many health benefits. We are designed to be in the sun but just not for HOURS at a time. Most people who live in cooler climates are deficient in vitamin D so it's worth investing in a quality supplement, particularly during the winter months (check out www.tristanlee.com/stuff for my latest product recommendations). Vitamin D can also be found in foods such as oily fish and eggs.

Pace Yourself in the Sun

It is much healthier to 'build up' your sun exposure gradually as your skin needs time to adjust if you've had many months of going without. This is particularly relevant on holiday when people literally 'fry' themselves in the sun. Sunburn is really painful, looks terrible (going to a job interview, date or party with bright red skin isn't a great way to make a good first impression), damages the skin and, in extreme cases, can lead to skin cancer so please, please be careful in the sun.

Use Sunscreen

UVA, UVB, SPF. Factor 20, 50, 100? What to choose? Selecting suntan lotion can be very confusing.

There are two different types of ultraviolet rays in sunlight:

1. UVA are the rays that age the skin (A for ageing)
2. UVB are the rays that burn the skin (B for burning)

Therefore, look for a sunscreen that offers protection from both. This is sometimes referred to as 'broad spectrum'. For most people, their skin will start to burn after about ten minutes of full sun exposure without any protection. SPF 20, for example, will provide 20 times the protection of no sunscreen i.e. 200 minutes or just over three hours. The sun protection numbers aren't an exact science so it's best to re-apply every couple of hours or more if swimming, sweating or exercising. In hot weather, SPF 30 is the best option for the majority of people.

Although black/brown skin has built-in sun protection as it contains far higher levels of melanin, it is still prone to burning if exposed to excessive amounts of sunshine, especially after the winter months of little or no sun.

I am a big fan of wearing sun hats. Your face is the part of your body that gets the most sun exposure so it is advisable to protect it. I recommend a light-coloured hat (that reflects the sun's rays) with a wide brim that keeps your face and entire neck in the shade rather than heaping loads of sunscreen on your face and having to regularly re-apply. So, by all means, enjoy the sunshine, but also respect it. As with everything in life, moderation is the key.

Tip #19
Skincare: Face-ing the Truth

Your skin is your largest organ and as such it's essential to keep it in tip-top condition. Both your face and body need to be looked after properly. People have certainly got better at taking care of their complexions but more often than not they completely neglect their skin from the neck down. By thoroughly cleansing your entire body you'll not only look gorgeous, but smooth, hydrated skin from head to toe is also very youthful. From face wash, face and body scrubs to face and body lotions, being gorgeous inside and out involves the need for an overall approach to looking good and feeling great.

Face: The Facts

Our faces are the part of us that we most expose to the world. They are our calling card. Even though the face makes up only a small percentage of our body, it's the part of us that is always on display. Yet, most people spend more time and money on their mobile phones than on taking care of their skin. Looked after properly, your skin can look great for your entire life. Sadly, not everyone is blessed with a flawless, smooth complexion that glows with health and vitality, but the good news is that you can significantly improve the condition of your skin without it costing a lot of time or money.

If you're new to skin-care, be patient and be prepared to commit at least three weeks to establish a routine. From my experience of helping people over the years, once you start you'll never look back. It takes only a small amount of effort to see significant results. Not only will you see a marked improvement in the quality and texture of your skin but taking care of your appearance also does wonders for your confidence and self-esteem. So, what are you waiting for? Go on, get stuck in.

All Washed Up?

It always surprises me that a lot of people I talk to don't actually wash their faces properly. If you're under the impression that just splashing your face with some warm water in the shower each morning is cleansing your face thoroughly, this isn't the case. Water alone does not actually remove dirt, dead skin cells and the effects of pollution. At the opposite end of the spectrum, using shower gel to wash your face is equally as ineffective. Most shower gels are highly fragranced and therefore aren't designed to be used on the face. Also, many of the 'sports' shower gels have deodorising ingredients that, if used on the delicate face area, can dry out the skin and potentially cause irritation.

Why Wash Your Face in the First Place?

Your face is the part of you that is most exposed to the elements so treat it with the respect it deserves. Taking care of your face can make a massive difference to your appearance.

Here are my six top tips for clean, gorgeous skin:

1. Do NOT use shower gel on your face – ever!
2. Use a mild, foaming face wash twice a day: morning and evening.
3. Wash your face after exercise to minimise the chances of spots developing.
4. Wash your hands in the shower first as this removes any oil from the surface of your hands so your face wash can lather more effectively.
5. It's better to use a little bit of face wash twice than a lot of product once. This is called 'double cleansing'.
6. Don't forget to wash your entire neck too as most people completely ignore this area.

Washing your face effectively morning and evening is the the cornerstone of great skincare. If you do nothing else, make sure that you cleanse your face to keep your complexion looking fresh, healthy and sexy.

Tip #20

Face Scrubs: Go from Drab to Fab

Face scrubs are a great way to remove (exfoliate) dead skin cells from the surface of the skin therefore brightening and freshening the complexion. In a nutshell, a face scrub is a cream with little 'bits' in it and when applied to the face in a gentle, circular motion helps to transform tired, dull skin. For guys, using face scrubs in the shower before shaving is really useful as it 'wakes up' your stubble helping to prevent ingrown hairs.

Six golden rules for face-scrub success:

1. Use twice a week at least.
2. NEVER apply to the delicate under-eye area or if you have sun-burnt or damaged skin.
3. Avoid overly-perfumed or medicated products as they can irritate the skin, especially the sensitive neck area.
4. Be cautious if you have spots or cuts.
5. Use a 20p-sized amount and divide this between your forehead, cheeks, chin, nose and neck before gently rubbing in.
6. Be gentle: You're not sanding floorboards.

Using a face scrub is a fantastic way to significantly

brighten your complexion especially during the winter months. It can invigorate your skin and help you glow with health and vitality. Youthful looking skin is just a face-scrub away.

For my latest product recommendations, go to www.tristanlee.com/stuff

Bonus Section
Eye, Eye: What a Great Eye-dea!

The skin under the eye area is the thinnest on the entire body and as such needs to be treated with extra care. For most people, this is the area that first develops signs of ageing i.e. wrinkles. Therefore, taking care of this delicate region is important to delay the effects of premature ageing.

Here are my five top tips for eye-mazing eye care:

1. Use a moisturiser which contains an SPF minimum factor 15. Use this every day, all year round to minimise the ageing effects of UV light. During hot weather re-apply sunscreen to this area or simply wear a sun hat.

2. Use an under-eye cream or rich moisturiser before you go to bed. The skin repairs itself at night so give it a helping hand.

3. Don't apply product too near the eye but just underneath it to avoid getting any in the eye.

4. For tired eyes and to reduce puffiness, use slices of chilled cucumber or used tea-bags that have been left to cool. Lie down, place on the eyes and relax for a couple of minutes.
5. Avoid excessively rubbing your under-eye area as this can damage the skin.

Prevention is better than a cure, so protect this delicate area and you'll look younger and fresher for longer.

Tip #21
(Face)Pack Up Your Troubles

Face packs are a great way of deep cleansing and rejuvenating the face and giving it some much-needed T.L.C. (Tristan Loving Care)

There are two main types:

Clay: As the name suggests this product contains clay which is a really effective way of removing excess oil from the skin. If you have spots or oily areas then this product is ideal for you to use.

Hydrating: As opposed to clay masks that effectively take oil away, using a hydrating mask is great if you have a dry complexion as it puts moisture back into the skin which makes it look healthy and fresh.

My Five Face Pack Golden Rules

1. Always wash skin thoroughly with a gentle, foaming face wash before using a face pack.
2. Lightly dampen the face and spread a small (walnut size) amount evenly over the entire face, including the neck area (and the back of the neck if you have more time). Do not use clay masks on the delicate under eye area.
3. Leave on the skin for 5-10 minutes and rinse off

thoroughly using a damp flannel or small face sponge. If using a clay mask (which will dry hard), splash the face several times with warm water first to 'loosen' up the mask before removing. This avoids excessively rubbing the skin to remove the product which can aggravate it.

4. Use twice a week for a face treat.
5. It's far better to apply a face pack at the bathroom sink rather than in the shower.

Clay face packs are a great way to draw out impurities from the skin. You may find that this may result in the occasional spot but do not be alarmed as this is simply your skin getting rid of toxins. Try to avoid using just before a big occasion in case you have an adverse reaction.

Top Money-Saving Tip:

If you're looking for a really effective, natural and very inexpensive way to hydrate your skin, then coconut oil is the way to go. On freshly-cleansed skin, cover your face, neck (and back of your hands if you're feeling adventurous) with a teaspoon of coconut oil, leave for five minutes and rinse off using a fresh flannel and warm water. Splash with cold water and pat dry with a clean towel. And, voila, gorgeously soft and hydrated skin. Choose raw, organic coconut oil for best results.

Product Recommendations:

Low price: organic coconut oil

Medium price: Dr Organic (four varieties: Manuka honey, Rose Otto, Virgin Olive Oil and Charcoal)
Higher price: Dermalogica skin hydrating masque

For my latest and most favourite product recommendations, go to www.tristanlee.com/stuff

Tip #22
Rub-A-Dub-Dub, Some Moisturiser in a Tub

I am a massive fan of using moisturiser. I have used some EVERY day since I was 18 years old. My 29-year love affair with moisturiser has been the most satisfying and rewarding relationship I've ever had. These days people are generally happy to use a moisturiser. When I was a teenager there was very little to choose from but thankfully these days there's an enormous variety of products available for us all to get our hands on. Despite the fact that people are buying face creams, I have discovered through the workshops I deliver as well as the one-to-one coaching sessions I conduct that a lot of people are unsure how to actually apply moisturiser properly.

When applying moisturiser there are two main methods that I use:

1. The 'rub together and smear all over' method: This method is the quick and basic approach to putting on moisturiser and helps to give an even amount of product coverage to the face and neck. This technique is most effective if you're in a rush and/or have 'normal' skin. Gently place a walnut-sized amount in the palm of your hands, simply apply the moisturiser evenly all over the face and gently rub in until the cream disappears.

2. The 'scoop and dab' method: This approach is my preferred one. It is more 'targeted' as it helps you to apply moisturiser only where needed e.g. forehead, under eye, cheeks and neck. By squeezing a walnut-sized amount of product into one hand (like an artist's palette) and then using a couple of fingertips on the other hand 'scoop and dab' the moisturiser onto your face. The beauty of this approach is that you can apply more to dry areas and less to oily ones. If you have oily skin on your nose only apply a tiny amount to this area. Perhaps none at all if your nose is particularly greasy.

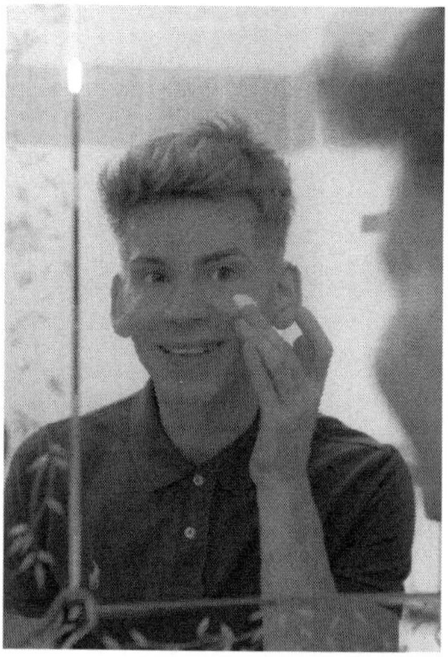

Here are six extra bonus moisturising tips for maximum gorgeousness

1. Select a moisturiser that doesn't contain harsh chemicals or preservatives and which contains an SPF of at least factor 15.

2. Use it every day, even in winter, to protect your face from the damaging effects of UV light.
3. Always wash your face before applying moisturiser.
4. When applying moisturiser, gently stretch and move your face to give your muscles a bit of a workout. Exaggerating these movements will help to keep you looking younger, sexier for longer and increase blood flow to the face.
5. Your neck is exposed to the elements and therefore potential sun damage so apply a small amount to the BACK as well as the front of your neck. For women, it's important to apply sun cream and moisturiser to the décolletage as it's susceptible to sun damage and wrinkles. Also, don't forget to apply a small amount to each hand.
6. Apply a small amount to the tips of your ears if they are exposed especially during hot weather.

My goal is to encourage everyone to start using moisturiser properly. A lot of people I speak to are under the misguided notion that moisturisers can give you spots or that if you have oily skin you should avoid using any lotion on your face. This is simply untrue. By choosing a product that suits your skin type and applying it effectively you can have a healthy, hydrated and gorgeous complexion. People will literally stop you in the street and marvel at your glowing skin.

Tip #23

Pain in the Neck

As your Guardian of Gorgeousness, I'd like to talk about a serious topic that's close to my heart (well nearer my head actually): and that is the neck. I may be putting my neck on the line but I'll press forwards regardless.

You may think that this part of your body is simply the bit that connects your body to your head and have never given it much thought – until now. We need to change this. Apart from the occasional love bite or attention from vampires, your poor old neck is generally completely ignored. My mission is to stand up for necks everywhere and explain that neck-glecting this area can be a recipe for all sorts of unpleasant consequences. So, it's time to stick your neck out and give it the attention it so rightly deserves.

Although most people now realise that taking care of their face is a worthwhile endeavour, the vast majority of people don't appreciate that the neck is actually part of the face. Your face doesn't end at your jawline. Who knew? I understand that this is a startling fact so if you need to sit down for a couple of minutes to gather your thoughts before reading on then please take this opportunity to do so.

Two minutes later….

Your face (including your neck) is the part of you that is most on show and exposed to the elements and therefore needs to be treated accordingly. On a daily basis, this area is subject to pollution, dirt, heat, rain, UV light and all manner of environmental (external) factors that can adversely affect your skin.

Have you ever seen a happy, clean and moisturised face sitting on top of a sad, wrinkly and saggy neck? Let's be honest, it's not a pretty sight. You may laugh but this could be your future if you don't take action immediately. Here's another mind-blowing fact: Your neck is circular and isn't just the area directly under your chin but it actually goes all the way around. Not since Ferdinand Magellan proved the world was round rather than flat over 500 years ago has a revelation had such a profound effect on humankind. Okay, okay, maybe I'm exaggerating a little, but it's important.

So, let's get down to business. Here are my three top tips for nice necks:

1. When you wash your face, don't forget your neck and BACK of the neck.

2. The same applies for moisturiser: Use product on the front and back of your neck.

3. Finally, when using sunscreen make sure ALL of your neck gets a dollop of SPF. Guys tend to have short hairstyles, leaving the back region of the neck

exposed and vulnerable to UV damage. Alternatively, wear a wide-brimmed sun hat to keep your face and neck (particularly back of the neck) in the shade. For guys, cricket hats provide excellent coverage and look sporty, so it's a win-win situation.

You can dramatically reduce wrinkles and other signs of premature ageing by treating your neck with respect. No more neck-neglect okay? I'll be watching. My N.N.H. (Neck Neglect Hotline) will be going live soon so you can report any neck neglect crimes you encounter.

Tip #24
(Coco)-nuts About Coconut Oil

Coconut oil hydrates and nourishes your skin and has anti-ageing and anti-oxidant properties (i.e. protects against wrinkles and fine lines). Our faces are a bit like a wooden dining table: From time to time they need 'oiling' to keep them looking their best. The coconut oil I buy costs anywhere from £5-£12 and lasts ages as a small amount goes a really long way. For my latest and most favourite product recommendations, go to www.tristanlee.com/stuff.

Coconut oil is a must-have, multi-purpose product and as such I absolutely love it. It really is the eighth wonder of the world and has more uses than Mr Very Useful from Usefulville.

1. You can cook with it.
2. You can use it as a butter/margarine substitute for spreading on bread, rice cakes or crackers.
3. Most exciting of all, it can be used on your face and body as it contains vitamin E.

It may initially feel a bit strange that one minute you're spreading it on your toast and the next you're putting it on your face, but trust me, once you get over the initial shock you'll be a life-long fan. Also, it has a pleasant, subtle coconut scent and it's solid in its natural state.

Like many things that are new to any market, coconut oil does have some detractors, and of course, you should make your own mind up about this.

Why Cook with Coconut Oil?

Coconut oil has a unique composition of fatty acids and is rich in health-boosting lauric acid. It is also resistant to high heat and is far better for cooking than olive oil. Coconut oil will turn into liquid form if the temperature rises above 24 degrees centigrade so be warned: It can change consistency. If you prefer not to use it in melted form (as I do) simply stick it in the fridge for a few minutes until it sets. I think it works better solid as it is more economical and easier to use.

For Use on the Face and Body

This amazing product normally comes in a glass jar so for practical purposes I would suggest scooping four heaped tablespoons into a plastic container with a watertight lid so if your coconut oil does melt then it won't spill everywhere. If possible, try to keep it flat whilst storing.

How to Use:

Face

You only need a TINY amount to achieve a great result. Using a mirror, dab some coconut oil onto your index finger (hopefully this encourages you not to use too much) and apply to your face in gentle strokes. Remember: Always wash your face first using a gentle foaming face wash to open the pores so that the oil is absorbed. Coconut oil is particularly effective for the under-eye area, dry patches and for men on the neck area after they've shaved. Spend a couple of minutes gently massaging it in before you apply your moisturiser. It's great on dry hands too.

You will find that because you've applied coconut oil, you'll need less moisturiser therefore saving money.

Body

I love using coconut oil on my whole body once a week or whenever my skin is dry. Once again you don't need very much. Use a small amount and apply to dry areas, especially knees, elbows and anywhere else that takes your fancy. Your skin will glow with health and you'll smell gorgeous too.

What Type of Coconut Oil to Buy?

I recommend buying an unrefined/raw, organic brand. There are several great brands available in health food stores and if you're just using it on your face it will last for ages. It's exceptional value for money.

For my latest and most favourite product recommendations, go to www.tristanlee.com/stuff.

Conclusion

Thanks to social media and more scrutiny from the press, we are all a little more aware of some of the harsh and potentially harmful ingredients contained in many of the beauty products we use every day. From shampoo to toothpaste, what you choose to put in your hair, under your armpits and spread over your face and body can sometimes be more like chemical warfare than pampering. However, because coconut oil is completely natural you can relax, safe in the knowledge that there are no nasty side-effects. If it's okay to eat then it's fine to use on your face and body.

Tip #25
Hand-some Hands

Hands up if you completely neglect your hands? Do not fear, you are not alone. Despite the fact that our hands work really hard for us they generally get very little thanks. From the harsh chemicals used in washing-up liquid to exposure to the ageing effects of UV light as well as a whole host of other environmental factors, our hands, because they are constantly on show, are particularly vulnerable to damage. Real gorgeousness means understanding that the state of your hands is important especially as good hand-care creates a positive first impression. If you suffer from tough, weathered skin or cracked fingernails then this section is for you.

Hand-le With Care

Have you ever been on a bus or tube and seen someone biting their nails like they've never eaten before? Well, I have and it is a very unpleasant habit that we should grow out of by the age of five. However, a lot of adults still do this.

Chewed, infected fingernails are not only horrible to look at but can also give off the impression of someone who doesn't care about their appearance. I appreciate that many people chew their nails as a nervous habit, a bit like grinding your teeth. Try using 'Stop & Grow' which is a product you can put on your nails to help you stop biting them – because it tastes so bad.

> For my latest and most favourite product recommendations, go to www.tristanlee.com/stuff.

Aside from your face, your hands are the part of you that are most on show to the world so it makes sense to take care of them. You can tell a lot about someone from the state of their hands. Well-looked after hands and nails demonstrate positive character attributes and poor hand care indicates the opposite. Running a close second to foot care, the hands are generally neglected by most people.

Here are my eight top hand-y tips for hand-some hands:

1. After showering, clean fingernails EVERY day with a pointed nail file or nail brush. When fingernails are soft they are far easier to clean.

2. Trim fingernails every couple of weeks with nail clippers. Use a nail file to smooth away rough edges.

3. Protect hands from harsh chemicals by wearing rubber gloves or using barrier cream when using cleaning products.

4. Avoid over-using anti-bacterial hand wash as this can dry out the skin.

5. Use hand lotion after showering and doing the washing up.
6. When applying SPF moisturiser to your face, add some to your hands to protect them from the ageing effects of UV light as your hands are also constantly exposed to the sun too.
7. During the winter, give your hands extra love and attention as cold weather can dry and crack delicate skin.
8. Treat yourself to a professional manicure on a regular basis, or at least as an occasional treat when you can afford it.

Hands up for great hands. I'm handing you all you need for gorgeously hand-some hands on a plate. Okay, I'll be more hands-off with the hand jokes now!

Tip #26

Anyone for Skin and Tonic?

These days there's a lot of talk about skincare within the beauty industry. However, books, magazines and websites mostly offer advice on all aspects of how to take care of your face. It's true to say that the vast majority of your skin isn't on your face at all but on your body. Just because your face is on show more than your body (unless you are a stripper), it doesn't mean that you should neglect taking care of it. Have you ever seen people who have obviously invested time and money taking care of the skin on their face but have completely ignored the skin on their body? Well, I have and it's not a good look. The skin is your largest organ and keeping it in tip-top condition has health as well as cosmetic benefits. So, when we think of skincare we ought to be concerned with the entire body.

Here are my five tip tops for glowing skin:

1. Shower Gel: The cornerstone of great skin is keeping it clean. So, wash it daily with a mild shower gel. It always surprises me that a lot of people only wash their 'pits and bits'. You may not have the time to clean your entire body every day but make sure you do so at least three times a week. Or simply make some time by spending five minutes less on Facebook?

2. Body Scrub: To achieve healthy, glowing skin all over, using a body scrub or exfoliating sponge is a must. In the same way that a face scrub helps to remove dead skin cells, using a body scrub or exfoliating sponge can transform the appearance and texture of the skin on your body. Pay particular attention to knees and elbows. As a general rule, body scrubs contain larger 'bits' in order to effectively smooth and polish. As the skin on your body is thicker than your face you can treat it a little rougher and apply more pressure when using this product. Body scrubs should not be used on the face.

3. Body Lotion: Most people have come to terms with using a moisturiser on their face but using a lotion on their bodies can be an alien concept. In the same way that moisturising your face helps to protect it, keep it hydrated and give your face a healthy glow, moisturising your body has the same effect. So why do most people not get this result? There are three main reasons:

    i. Laziness.
    ii. Using the wrong product.
    iii. Using too much product.

There is a belief that body lotion can feel too heavy on your skin. This can be true if you choose a lotion that's too rich for your skin type and if you use too much. If you have dry skin, use a creamier lotion and if your skin is oily then use a lighter lotion. The key is only using a small amount, for example, a walnut-sized amount per leg, the same amount should do for both arms.

4. Diet/Water/Lifestyle: Your diet and the amount of water you consume will show up on your skin. A healthy lifestyle will help your skin to repair itself effectively. So, drink up (water, that is) and your skin will thank you for it. Exercise is also incredibly beneficial for skin health as it stimulates blood flow to the surface, increases circulation and keeps the skin toned and taut. It also reduces sagging.
5. Sun Safety: The main cause of poor-quality body skin is sun damage. If you've ever seen older people who have spent too much time sunbathing (or on sun-beds), you'll know what I mean: very wrinkly, thickened skin. What I would call LHS – Leather Handbag Syndrome. Saggy brown skin is the result of too much time spent roasting in the sun without adequate sun protection. Many of the wrinkles we associate with ageing are caused by sun damage. The good news is that this is preventable. Be safe in the sun. Avoid excessive amounts of sun exposure during the hottest time of the day (ordinarily 12pm-3pm) and regularly re-apply sunscreen or find a shady spot.

Your body skin, if cared for properly, can look great for a lifetime so now that you know what to do there's no excuse not to have sexy, smooth and supple skin that people will want to touch and caress.

Tip #27
Why Con-Tris-tency is the Key to Gorgeousness

The key to achieving the best results from any product, whether it's a face wash, a body scrub or moisturiser, is to use it regularly. In an ideal world, you could use a product once and the effects would last forever. However, this is sadly not the case.

A lot of people will use a face wash for a couple of weeks but then stop before a true habit has had the chance to be established. Why is this? We are all naturally impatient and want quick fixes and easy solutions, yet taking care of your face and body takes time and requires a life-long commitment. I have been washing and moisturising my face twice a day, EVERY day since I was 18. That's 29 years of discipline and investment. It's now such a part of my life that I can't imagine NOT doing it. For me, it is never a chore, rather it's something I really enjoy. It's 'me-time' and I find the process very relaxing, therapeutic and empowering.

The best way to form daily habits is to create and follow a self-care routine. It takes a while to establish a routine.

Experts now suggest it can take twenty-one to sixty-six days to form a habit.[26] So, commit to your new gorgeousness routine for at least a month until it has become second nature.

What Do I Mean by a Self-Care Routine?

For example, a morning self-care routine could look like this:

- Shower using shower gel
- Shampoo and condition hair
- Wash face with a mild face wash (in the shower)
- Clean finger and toenails with a pointed nail file
- Shave (for guys) at the bathroom sink
- Moisturise face (use a product that contains sun protection)
- Brush and floss teeth

An evening self-care routine could look like this:

- Wash and moisturise face, neck and hands
- Brush and floss teeth

---

[26] Dean, S. (2018). *Here's How Long It Really Takes to Break a Habit, According to Science*. Retrieved from https://www.sciencealert.com/how-long-it-takes-to-break-a-habit-according-to-science.

Popova, M. *How Long It Takes to Form a New Habit*. Retrieved from https://www.brainpickings.org/2014/01/02/how-long-it-takes-to-form-a-new-habit/

You can also add different elements to this routine:

- Twice a week use a face scrub
- Once a week use a face pack/mask
- Once a week use a body scrub or exfoliating sponge

The key is starting and being prepared to give it enough time for it to work. Trust me, the effort will be worth it. It's a great idea to try different products to see what works for you. Try not to jump in at the deep end and do everything all at once because for most people this simply isn't sustainable. Therefore, begin with using a face wash for a couple of weeks then add in a moisturiser and build in other products over time.

Planning

The French poet and writer Antoine de Saint-Exupery said, "A goal without a plan is just a wish" so it's worth considering what time of the day or evening works best for you. Ideally, give yourself more time than you would normally so you're not rushing. If you usually get ready in less than five minutes in the morning then give yourself 15 minutes, for example between 7am and 7.15. In the same way, if you normally go to sleep in front of the TV and then fall into bed at 2am then try doing your routine earlier in the evening, for example after dinner or before watching the news.

Before you know it, it will become a routine and you'll

love the way it makes you feel as well as look, so much so it'll be your favourite part of the day.

CHAPTER FOUR

CATEGORY: FEELINGS

Tip #28
The Motivation Myth

If you're missing motivation, don't worry, it's a myth anyway. Of all the topics I'm most often asked about, how to stay motivated features very highly.

So many of us are slaves to motivation and willpower. For years, I suffered the misery of 'feeling like' eating well, exercising or having a healthy lifestyle for only a few days or weeks only to run out of motivation. Then, when I stopped 'feeling like' doing it, I stopped like a car abruptly running out of fuel on a dual carriageway.

So, what do you do if you've broken down on the hard shoulder of life waiting for the AA to rescue you by delivering a huge dose of motivation? Do you resort to willpower?

Sometimes sheer determination can be really useful but it takes an enormous amount of energy to sustain that degree of discipline. If we rely on motivation to achieve and maintain our health and fitness goals, we can inadvertently set ourselves up for disappointment and failure.

Most people operate like this:

I feel motivated = I go to the gym, I prepare a healthy meal

I feel demotivated = I vegetate on the sofa, I order a takeaway

Feelings, Who Needs Them?

Don't trust them too much as feelings come and go. So, here's my advice. Don't rely on motivation to get you where you want to go. This may sound radical but in my experience feeling motivated is like a soufflé: it's easily deflated. I simply don't trust motivation; it's let me down too many times. And willpower isn't much better as it comes and goes like sunshine during British summertime: It's never consistent for more than a couple of days. Far more effective is understanding the miraculous power of a bit of planning and creating a few positive habits and learning to take action even when you don't feel like it.

So, what could taking action look like in reality?

*You want to eat healthier...keep a fully stocked fridge of fresh ingredients.
*You want to get fitter...buddy up with a friend and create a regular exercise habit.
*You want to eat more vegetables...have them delivered to your door.
*You want to try healthier meals...try 'Gousto' or 'Hello Fresh' (they deliver fresh meal ingredients to your front door – check out www.tristanlee.com/stuff for my latest recommendations for food delivery as new ones may have emerged since publishing this book).

Regarding food deliveries – ideally we would be sourcing our own local produce and making everything from scratch, but this isn't realistic for many people, so having the ingredients for lovely, filling meals delivered to your door with step-by-step instructions on how to cook, is a great plan B.

It may not be as exciting as the rush of adrenaline that usually accompanies motivation but taking the well-known fable of 'The Tortoise and the Hare' as an example, despite the hare getting off to a flying start it was the plodding tortoise who won the race.

For years, I was the hare making a spectacular start to a new fitness and healthy eating programme but always crashing and burning from not pacing myself. Getting fit and creating new food habits takes time, so slow down and give yourself more time to achieve the results you desire. Be like Michelangelo when he created 'David', which is probably the most celebrated sculpture in the history of art...consistently chip away at sculpting your own masterpiece. We are all a gorgeous work in progress so pace yourself, commit to seeing it through, focus on small daily habits to constantly improve yourself and relax and enjoy the journey.

It's really important not to give up when you stop, cheat or mess up. The key to long-term success is not making mistakes mean anything. Just dust yourself down, take a deep breath and get back on track.

> "Perfectionism is the enemy of progress." – Winston Churchill

A few daily brush strokes over time makes a far more beautiful painting than throwing a whole tin of paint onto a canvas. Replace the effort willpower requires with the ease of forming those few positive, daily habits.

Human beings have an enormous need for immediate results and yet this can be unrealistic and often really damaging. Lasting success isn't a race, it takes time so pace yourself.

Tip #29
Sharing Your Feelings

Take off your emotional corset, twirl it around your head and chuck it in the bin. Why? Because being 'buttoned up' didn't work for the Victorians and probably isn't working for you. So, here's how to pack up your troubles...

Most people are familiar with the phrase 'a problem shared is a problem halved' but how many of us actually reveal our innermost thoughts and feelings on a regular basis? Madonna had it right when she encouraged, 'Express Yourself' (wearing a cone-shaped bra is optional).

Whilst writing about and pondering upon the challenges of getting older, I am reminded of a client of mine who, for reasons of anonymity I'll call Phil, who is 46 years old.

Before my first one-to-one coaching call with him, I sent him a few questions to find out his goals and where he was coming from emotionally as well as physically. One of the questions was 'How would you rate your current level of self-esteem out of 10?' His reply was a sad 3.

He wrote the following: "Everyone thinks I'm a really fun, outgoing guy, always smiling and helping other people. Everyone comes to me when they have problems but when I look in the mirror I actually hate what I see. I've come to realise that I have a very low opinion of myself."

It became very clear during our very first coaching call that Phil had always kept all his feelings to himself and had never shared his internal struggles with anyone.

The only thing I ever ask my clients is to promise to be honest with themselves and to me about how they feel as we take steps together to improve their physical and mental health by encouraging them to reach out and express themselves when challenges emerge.

In my experience, much of what we define as a crisis is a series of incidents that for whatever reason were left unchecked until, like a volcano, they blow up in your face. Sometimes as we get older we can shut down that part of ourselves that's suffering because we're afraid of being vulnerable, scared of rejection or don't want to deal with it. Sadly, a lot of us do not deal with, or at least acknowledge, the rumblings of a storm coming until the hurricane actually washes our house away. By sharing our feelings, we can deal with things as they occur rather than letting them build up.

I have taught myself over many years not to keep important feelings to myself but to find healthy outlets to get them off my chest as I know – to my peril – that unexpressed feelings can over time become extremely toxic.

If you're not used to talking about how you feel, do not fear, you are in the majority. Here are two simple methods that can help you build up your E.Y.M. (Express Yourself Muscle):

1. Daily check-in (by yourself): At an airport when you go through customs you are asked if you have 'anything to declare'. As much as I am often tempted to quote Oscar Wilde's "I have nothing to declare but my genius", I have managed (so far) to refrain.

   A couple of times a day, simply stop and ask yourself:

   i. "How do I feel right now? What's going on in my mind? Am I feeling stressed, sad, inspired, lonely, happy, apathetic, excited?"

   ii. "What's going on in my body? Am I tired, in pain, aching or sore anywhere?"

   This is a simple and highly effective way of building up a relationship with your physicality as well as your emotional feelings.

2. Postcard chats (with another person): This is something I encourage my clients to do whereby they call me whenever they need a 'postcard chat'. This is a very short conversation where they briefly tell me about i) A challenging situation ii) How they feel. I offer a listening ear, a big dose of reassurance and some words of wisdom if necessary. The simple act of sharing how you feel is often enough to make

you feel better, lighter and less burdened. Developing the habit of reaching out, ideally as soon as something challenging happens, is essential to maintaining good long-term mental health. When you tell someone how you're feeling, the negative feelings either become less acute or sometimes completely disappear.

Conclusion

Many emotional challenges can be significantly reduced or even avoided altogether by adopting a proactive rather than a reactive approach to noticing, acknowledging and sharing your feelings with a trusted friend, close family member or a trained counsellor. I used to find it very difficult and often painful to share with others when I was having a tough time but being aware of the extremely negative consequences of not doing so (mental angst and physical ailments), I made a commitment to share anyway. I gradually got better with practice and now there's no stopping me. So, it's time to flex your E.Y.M. – starting today.

Tip #30
Expanding Your Comfort Zone (Gradually)

My mobile phone rings, I don't recognise the number but I pick up anyway:

"Hello!"

A voice says: "Hi, Mr Lee, it's your local A&E department calling. We have your comfort zone here and it's in a bit of a mess. It's been overly-stretched too quickly I'm afraid."

It seems everywhere we turn we are encouraged to expand our comfort zones, to triumph over our limited thinking and to generally make dramatic changes in our lives in order to be healthy, happier and more successful.

A case in point is our new year's health and fitness resolutions. We tend to enthusiastically over-indulge during the festive season only to attempt to spectacularly change how we eat, drink and move overnight once January 1st arrives. To drastically go from a Christmas diet to a summer diet during the middle of winter is rarely successful. It is far better to work with the seasons and make small, easy changes to your food and fitness over time by ramping up towards spring and summer when you'll naturally want to eat lighter meals and move more.

I'm a very big fan of making a commitment to carry out positive changes in our lives but I do feel that the 'all-or-nothing mentality' can be setting ourselves up for failure and frustration. It's really important to enlarge our comfort zone but I believe that just like a balloon if you expand it too quickly it'll burst.

The key to success is to make a gradual transition. We are often in a hurry but by slowing down a little, you'll develop habits that will set you up for long-term sustainable success rather than short-term wins.

I think of it this way: Rather than sorting out the cluttered garage in one day, sort out a box every day until the job is done. When something seems like a big deal, feels like it requires an enormous amount of effort or seems very challenging, the vast majority of us will feel scared, overwhelmed and will procrastinate. It's preferable for most people to attempt that new thing, or that task that's unfamiliar, to regularly dip your toe in the water to get used to the temperature rather than jumping right in.

Human nature hates nothing more than the unknown and uncertainty. So, if you sometimes give yourself a really hard time for not being motivated, focused or strong-willed enough to tackle the things that you want, don't. We are programmed from a young age to resist the unfamiliar. Our subconscious mind runs a mile from anything that exists outside of what we already know. So, I believe the best way is to 'trick' our mind into expanding our comfort zone very slowly so as not to shock it so violently that we immediately run back to safety, even if safety isn't good for you.

It's crazy but human beings will generally choose familiar misery over unfamiliar happiness every single time. Expanding your comfort zone too quickly can be overwhelming so no wonder we sometimes completely freak out (or is it just me?).

For example, would you rather go for a 10-minute walk twice a week for a month and double that every six months or go for a 10-mile walk seven days a week and double that every month? The first option is achievable, and I believe setting realistic, small goals over a long period of time is the best way to expand your comfort zone, particularly when you make it fun and break it down into bite-sized chunks. So, blow up that balloon slowly. Give yourself loads of time to achieve your goals and I guarantee you'll look back in a couple of years with a comfort-zone that has got substantially bigger.

Tip #31
Living in the Past

"I live in the past so much, I've had my post redirected there." – Tristan Lee

A sure-fire way to make getting older a miserable, frustrating and unhappy process is to dwell on the past. It seems to be common practice for people in their 40s, 50s and beyond to waste an enormous amount of time and energy thinking and reliving past upsets and traumas, as well as reminiscing. How often have you heard people say that "life was better then", or refer to "the best days of my life", or reminisce "if only I was 20 again."

Mid-life is naturally a time of reflection, contemplation and taking stock as we transition from the first half of our lives into the second. This process can be incredibly useful and rewarding when used in the right way.

At the end of each year I take myself off to a coffee shop and spend an hour or so answering these five questions:

What were the highlights of this year?
What were the challenges?
What did I learn from the challenges?
What am I most proud of?
What can I do differently next year?

My advice for minimising the difficulties often associated with getting older is to look at the past for reference rather than residence. Casually glancing over your shoulder and using the past to learn valuable lessons that can be implemented in the present and the future is far better than pitching up your tent in the past and stubbornly remaining there.

Would you prefer to carry a heavy stone, dragging you down and stopping you from moving on with your life, or to theatrically throw that stone to the ground, jump on a trampoline and let it propel you forwards? Well, when we spend too much time reminiscing about past regrets, or refer to times we were hurt or let down, it can rob us of enjoying our lives right now. It's human nature to ruminate (dictionary definition: rumination is the focused attention on the symptoms of one's distress, and on its possible causes, as opposed to solutions) so it does require awareness and some discipline to change this habit.

What are your thoughts about the future? Be honest. Are you excited, worried or do you not think about it at all? We have no control over what has happened so practice letting negative feelings about the past go. This isn't an easy thing to do as Christine, a client of mine, explains (name changed for anonymity):

"After a painful divorce and some serious health

challenges, I felt I no longer had much hope for the future because I was caught up living in the past. I made a decision to start taking care of my health, fitness and valuing myself more. It took a bit of time but I'm now daring to focus on future plans and allowing myself to be excited about what I can create rather than being dragged down by dwelling on past hurts and challenging experiences."

More goals are ruined, dreams destroyed and hopes dashed by letting the past dictate our future than anything else. So, next time you find yourself mulling over the past give yourself 15 seconds before you click your fingers and say out loud, "Okay! Time to move on."

What you focus on expands:

If you believe your past challenges determine your future, they will.
If you believe your best days are behind you, they will be.
If you believe you can learn lessons from the past to improve your future, you will.
If you believe some of your best days are still ahead, they shall be.

We need to be careful about what we think and focus on as we have a nasty habit of becoming what we most think about. So, jog towards the future while enjoying the journey by stopping occasionally to 'smell the roses'. Use the past to propel you forwards and to empower you to grow. The alternative is that we begin to shrink, to play small, to protect ourselves from being hurt and feeling disappointed or simply uncomfortable. I know what sounds like a better path to take. What about you?

Tip #32
Listen to Your Body

On my front door, I have a sign which reads: "Doorbell not working. Please knock. Hard!" It's been broken for about two years so maybe I should get it fixed, but I keep putting it off.

In the same way, as we get older we should be aware when our health doorbell isn't working and there's a knock on the door. For the vast majority of serious illnesses, there are warning signs and symptoms that if noticed and acted upon speedily could prevent them from becoming serious or even fatal.

As we get older, being in touch with how our bodies typically feel is essential so that we'll notice when we feel out of sorts.

The world's oldest piano tuner:

There was once a renowned piano tuner called Jacob who worked up until he died at the ripe old age of 102. When asked on his 100th birthday what the secret to his long career and even longer healthy lifespan was, he answered:

"As a piano tuner, I was taught to listen. I became an expert listener. After many years of training, I developed the ability to notice when a piano was slightly off-key or out of tune and then corrected it. I applied that skill to my own health. If I felt off-key or not hitting the right notes, I paid attention and made an effort to get retuned."

Women are generally more in touch with their bodies than men; however, the vast majority of people have no idea what's going on inside their bodies. We can get so used to certain aches and pains that we hardly even notice them anymore. The key is to avoid becoming complacent when something isn't quite right. We need, therefore, to develop a personal understanding of what our 'normal' is. By having a better relationship with our bodies, we can take appropriate action if necessary.

The key here is not to bury your head in the sand. Cemeteries are already full of people who didn't respond to early warning signs and I don't want you to join them. If you're someone who procrastinates about making an appointment with a doctor or other healthcare professional then my advice is to phone a good friend to ask them to pester you until you've made that appointment. I suggest that we all learn from Jacob and be in tune with our bodies so that our health can be a concerto.

Tip #33
Healthy Habits

"Depending on what they are, our habits will either make us or break us. We become what we repeatedly do."

– Steven Covey

We can't control our circumstances but we can control our habits.

As we get older, there are many things that seem to be out of our control, for example, bereavement, redundancy, divorce, issues with children and many more challenges, which can seriously impact our lives.

Over many years of helping people during the ups and downs of life, I have found that identifying the habits that promote emotional as well as physical vitality can really help to empower us to cope during times of stress or upheaval. I realised a few years ago that the quality of the daily habits I keep is the key to success in every area of my life, particularly when it comes to food and fitness. It's the small, and at first glance seemingly insignificant, actions and disciplines we commit to each day that matter the most.

Hopefully, we are all aware that the amazing benefits of taking on healthy habits are that they get easier if you keep doing them consistently. It simply takes less energy to continue with a new behaviour if we make it an integral part of our lives; it is 'simply what we do' and we don't really have to think about it. What things do you already do automatically every day? Here are some possible examples: eat breakfast, brush your teeth, use your mobile phone, check your emails, shower (hopefully) as well as many more. Up for a challenge? Why not identify and make a list of five habits that are supporting your long-term health and happiness and five habits that aren't.

Here are five of mine:

1. I always have a healthy breakfast.
2. I always have a fridge full of healthy food.
3. I put my exercise in my diary and make this a top priority.
4. I have good quality water with me at all times.
5. I make sure I thoroughly wash and moisturise my skin each night before sleep.

Since we're friends now, I should really tell you my five habits that don't support long-term health. I know you won't judge me!

1. Spending too much time on social media.
2. Occasionally getting so hungry (and grumpy) that I choose convenience over optimum nutrition.
3. Napping too much.

4. Sometimes being impatient that success is taking a long time to achieve.
5. Drinking too much coffee.

Here's an idea for you: Working on this list could be something you share with a close friend, partner or success buddy, which in turn could help them analyse and self-improve too?

Positive:

1.
2.
3.
4.
5.

Negative:

1.
2.
3.
4.
5.

> *"Successful people aren't born that way. They become successful by establishing habits of doing things that unsuccessful people don't like to do."*
>
> – William Makepeace Thackeray

So, keep adding daily habits to remain happy and healthy for the long-term. I have, over many years, trained myself to be less of a product of my circumstances.

This is how it used to be:

A good day = go to the gym, eat well, feel happy.

A bad day = don't go to the gym, sit around feeling lethargic, eat a tub of Haagan Daaz ice-cream and generally feel as flat as a pancake.

Since I've identified and value my positive habits, they tend to remain in place despite what's going on in my life. I don't throw everything out the window during difficult circumstances. We do have a choice. In fact, these days I go the other way which I call the 'T.C.M.' (Tristan's Contrary Method).

Here's how it works...If I've had a bad day I'll cook an even healthier dinner or go to the gym for longer. Having spent so much of my 20s and 30s at the mercy of my feelings, I decided in my early 40s to no longer be a slave to my circumstances and flip it all around by doing the polar opposite of what I would normally do. As the old cliché goes, 'life isn't what happens but how we react to what happens.'

I've always been unconventional and a bit of a rebel...if a sign says 'no entry', I'll go in. If everyone walks one way, I enjoy going in the opposite direction. So, be a shepherd, not a sheep when faced with challenges and use the awesome power of tiny, positive habits to help you overcome any obstacle that life may hurl your way.

Here's an example of a positive yet challenging habit

I've taken on and how over time I made it an easy one to keep up: I used to spend a lot of money on takeaways because I couldn't be bothered to cook.

I realised that the main reason for this was:

1. I didn't think ahead and plan my meals at all.
2. My fridge was usually empty so there wasn't any food to cook with in the first place.
3. I now do a supermarket shop every Monday, have a vegetable box delivered and receive monthly supplies of nuts, seeds and other healthy foodstuffs which I bulk buy online. I also think ahead so I have a better idea of what I'm cooking. I now save a lot of money as I no longer eat takeaways, my diet is so much healthier and I enjoy cooking. There's always ups and downs when attempting to cement a habit but it's really important to quickly get back on the horse if you mess up.

Tip #34

Say No to Procrastination

We all procrastinate. From David Beckham to Oprah, even really successful people delay taking action sometimes. So, don't panic, you're not alone.

A little less conversation, a bit more action please...

By its very definition, the word priority means the most important thing, the activity at the very top of your 'to do' list. Ultimately, you can't have more than one priority. So, what's the one thing that's most important to you at the moment? Is there one single task that just isn't getting the required attention? From my experience, the main reason people procrastinate is simply that the job at hand seems too hard, too difficult or too overwhelming. This is particularly true when it comes to making changes to our health, fitness and lifestyle goals. I often hear statements like: "I just don't know where to start", "I don't know what to do" and, "It feels so difficult to get the ball rolling". My answer to these people is, "Just start where you are."

Most people are highly resistant to change, to the unfamiliar or to uncertainty so they put off doing that thing because they don't know what it looks like once the change is in place and instead choose 'not to get around to it' because it's more familiar. In a strange way, some human beings would prefer to be in their comfort zone and unhappy but safe rather than slightly out of their normal space and being happy.

The true story of Stan the procrastination man:

Stan, someone I know extremely well, really wanted to write a book. It had been an ambition of his for many years to share his life experiences in a fun self-help book but he kept delaying getting started and was feeling really miserable about it. Just the thought of writing a book made him come out in a cold sweat. One day while having coffee with his best friend, he confessed how frustrated and overwhelmed he was about not being able to write a book. His friend (who just happened to be a published author himself) grabbed a paper napkin and a pen and outlined a very simple plan with some loose deadlines. This plan involved taking a small number of realistic daily actions (just writing for an hour per day, for example). He then also offered to be Stan's accountability buddy. Suddenly, Stan felt like the fog had lifted and then clearly saw the way forward. Breaking the book-writing project down into small actions like writing for one hour every day, took an unachievable project and transformed it into one that he could slowly but surely make happen. Each day, Stan would commit to writing an hour a day and messaging his friend when he'd completed that action. A chart also helped his progress. Ticking a box each day was really motivating for him. So, what happened to the book, I hear you ask? Well, dear reader, you're holding it. (Stan is one of my nick-names. Tri-Stan!)

Procrastination can often feel like a heavy weight around our necks so firstly, make whatever you're not getting around to doing a priority. Then, take a step back and break down the job at hand into bite-sized, manageable chunks and draw up a simple plan. If you were going to eat an elephant (I don't advise it), you'd do so in small chunks.

Finally, ask someone for support and accountability by promising to text them once you've completed your promised action each day. I guarantee you'll be up and running in no time at all and feeling so light and happy you'll most likely float away like a helium balloon at a birthday party.

Tip #35
Apathy vs Tiredness

The phone rings, I answer "Hello, Chris!"

Chris: "I'm not going to go to the gym with you this evening as I just can't be bothered to be honest."

Me: "I'll pick you up and 7 pm and we'll just do a shorter session then. Bye." And then I hang up.

As Dolly Parton said, "It takes a lot of money to look this cheap." So, in the same way, I generally flip it around when my gym buddy says he can't be bothered because I know he most likely means something else, for example: "I'm bored of the routine we do" or "I'm a bit fed up at work" or "Something else has come up which is more appealing", or more often than not, "I'm not seeing the results I want quick enough."

Let me tell you a story...

About four years ago a good friend asked me what I wanted for Christmas. I replied, "Why don't you surprise me."

So, on Christmas Day I opened an envelope from him with a voucher for a six-part practical philosophy course in central London. My initial thought was that I should have asked for cash; however, I decided to take the plunge and try something different. I don't remember a great deal about the course apart from the explanation of apathy vs tiredness. A concept that I can only say was life-changing.

Before the course, I hadn't ever considered there was a difference between apathy and tiredness. Therefore, it was a revelation to me when it was proposed that apathy is a call to action whereas tiredness is a call to rest. I would define apathy as feelings of indecisiveness, a twitchy and restless energy. The conclusion being that if I ever hear myself utter the words "I can't be bothered", then it's actually a clue for me do something, to take action, to express that restless energy.

So, how does this apply to my day-to-day life? Here are three examples of me pushing through my apathy:

1. If I say I can't be bothered to cook...I cook (but possibly something quick and easy).
2. If I say I can't be bothered to go for a run...I go for a run (but possibly a shorter one than usual or a brisk walk).
3. If I can't be bothered to wash my face before bed....I do (but quickly to fun music).

On the other hand, if I'm actually feeling tired I will rest and this is because our daily energy levels fluctuate and are finite. In the same way that a mobile phone has only a few hours of battery life before it needs recharging, we do too. With that in mind, I do my best to use my energy on my priorities FIRST. Currently, my priorities are exercising daily, healthy eating and writing this book. Any energy left over I spend on activities that are not a priority. This helps me not get so tired that I don't want to work out or cook great food, and this is important to me because being fitter and eating nutritional food gives me more energy. So, choose how you use your precious energy really carefully and defend it vigorously if others try to steal it.

Apathy will never go away because it's part of being human, therefore, the key is to change the way we relate to it whenever it shows up…so that we don't let it stop us. Since I've become aware of how to distinguish the difference between apathy and tiredness (especially when it comes to my physical and emotional health and well-being), I've made sure that I CAN be bothered.

So, what one thing, dear reader, are you putting off? Remember, procrastination weighs you down, but action takes the weight off your shoulders. So why not take some action today? Go on, start with just one thing.

Tip #36
Man (or Woman) in the Mirror

How do you feel about your body? Are you constantly critical about certain body parts? Do you stare at yourself in a full-length mirror or at the gym and obsess about your 'muffin tops' or that your biceps aren't big enough? What do you say to yourself about your body?

There is a great deal of bodily dissatisfaction amongst people today. Over the past few years, there has been a massive increase in fitness magazines and underwear adverts portraying images of supposed perfection. Body dissatisfaction sells products. Despite the fact we all know that these are professional fitness models who spend hours in the gym each day, have a very disciplined lifestyle with regards to their diet and are airbrushed to make their six-packs stand out more, we still aspire to look like them. It's crazy!

We live in a society where comparing ourselves to others is an epidemic. If you ever hear yourself saying: "She's in better shape than me" or "He's got bigger biceps" or "I wish my stomach was as flat as hers", what you're actually saying is: "I'm not as good as them, therefore, I can't feel good about myself because I fall short of that ideal."

Don't get me wrong, I have bought into this as well. Yet, as

I get older I am trying to accept myself and focus on what I do like about myself. We cannot be others and they cannot be us. I do like fitness magazines but these days I tend to look at them less, as in many ways they promote low self-esteem. This isn't me being critical, as there is a lot of valuable content about lifestyle and nutrition in these publications – but at the same time the image of an ideal physique is promoted (even worshipped) and yet most people will never look like that.

So, without sounding too corny, I think we should start being kinder to our bodies. If there are things you don't like about yourself, you can still treat that part of your body with respect. For example, if you see that you have a bit of a belly but you're working towards eating better, cutting down on the booze and upping your exercise, then give yourself credit for what you are doing and stop putting yourself down. Respect and honour your body and it will do the same to you.

I am a huge fan of exercise as you do walk taller when you are in shape, your posture is better, clothes look better on you and it can do wonders for your confidence. Yet, if the emphasis is 100% on appearance rather than on how you feel, it can be unhelpful. These days I am fortunate to have a positive body image but this wasn't always the case. I'm not that tall, I have ginger hair, I have very pale skin and freckles. Oh, and a long body with short legs, but it's pointless wishing I was taller and had a radically different body.

I have learnt to say: "I'm glad I am the height I am. If I were taller none of my clothes would fit."

There are many examples of people dramatically transforming the way they look. We've all heard of skinny teenagers that were bullied at school, then spent years in the gym and became muscle-bound hunks, which is of course incredibly impressive. However, not everyone will be able to achieve such radical changes.

For me, the priority now is health, high self-esteem and balance. I have met plenty of people with incredible bodies but chasing perfection and focusing on this area alone can mean other areas can go underdeveloped, and these people can be quite unhappy.

We all want to feel the same things: to be accepted, loved, admired, approved of and that we belong, yet there are lots of ways to do this that don't involve spending four hours a day at the gym.

Some people who obsess about their bodies are really saying: "Please think I'm good enough, please think that I'm special." You are already special so there's no need to try so hard.

So, here's a practical tip: Next time you look in the mirror rather than hating yourself for not being perfect, be kind to yourself and say out loud: "I am a gorgeous work in progress. I am perfect in my imperfections. I will make gradual changes over time and give myself lots of encouragement and praise to feel good about myself on the journey."

> *"Learn to be happy with what you have while you pursue all that you want."*
>
> – Jim Rohn

By all means make changes to your fitness and body shape but rather than beating yourself with a stick, use that stick to lean on for support.

Tip #37

How to Put the Style Back into Lifestyle

A wise man said that without good health you have nothing and I happen to agree. You can be the most attractive person in the world with a flawless complexion and the body of a Greek God but that all counts for nothing if you're in poor health. Valuing your health is essential for anyone who aspires to look and feel their best. If your diet and overall lifestyle are terrible then no amount of moisturiser will compensate for not taking care of yourself properly.

From sleep to me-time, let's explore effective ways of maximising your health and vitality. If you're interested in making the most of your looks to improve your self-confidence or to simply be more sexually attractive, recognising that true youthfulness is an 'inside' job is the best place to start.

Stress, lack of sleep and pollution all contribute to us ageing before our time. Therefore, I encourage everyone to invest in me-time. A holistic approach to health and well-being is needed in order to live a happy, balanced life. So many people put themselves at the bottom of the list. Just because you're a busy person with a family to take care of and a job to do, it doesn't mean you should completely neglect yourself. You're of no use to anyone if you don't take care of your physical and emotional well-being. If you want to age well then prioritise opportunities to relax and unwind. Mowing the lawn, painting the lounge, building a tree house can wait, your health can't. It's so easy to be busy but what's more important? Answer: YOU.

The Benefits of Me-Time

As much as I think the stigma of people taking care of themselves has radically changed over the past few years, there is still room for improvement. Women have known for years about the benefits of a bit of 'me time', whether it's a hot soak in a tub, a pedicure or putting nice lotions on their skin. It's about time guys got in on the act too. Maybe you're too busy or feel guilty about spending time and money on yourself? Well, don't. Any effort you make will have multiple benefits on your life. Taking time to 'pamper' yourself can have a dramatic effect on your self-esteem as well as boosting your confidence and overall happiness.

How much time do you currently invest in yourself, your appearance or your health? If it is minimal then now is the time to start respecting the most important thing in the world: YOU.

Please answer the following questions.

Score yourself 1-10 (1 = never, 10 = all the time)

How often do you have a relaxing hot bath?
How often do you get a massage?
How often do you get lots of fresh air?
How often do you 'pamper' yourself?
How often do you exercise?
How often do you go for a walk?
How often do you make time to unwind and relax?
How often do you spend time alone in nature?
How often do you take 30 seconds to breathe deeply?
How often do you prioritise getting enough sleep?

How did you get on?

1-24...Oh dear, you're making yourself a low priority.
25-49...Room for improvement.
50-74...You're on your way, keep going.
75-100...Well done, you're really investing in you.

Isn't it fascinating that if our car isn't working we generally take it to the garage immediately? If you hear a rumbling in the engine off you go to have it looked at. The last thing you want is to ignore it as the whole car is seriously affected if the engine blows. Trust me, I know – it happened to me.

Sadly, a lot of people look after their cars better than their own health. By law your car needs to pass its MOT and have regular services, but why is it that the same rule doesn't apply to having our bodies checked out? This seems crazy.

Many diseases, if caught early enough, are very treatable. Prevention is always better than a cure. The idea of spending hundreds of pounds keeping prized automobiles in good condition is acceptable but the concept of investing in regular health check-ups is seen as a waste of money. Something is terribly wrong here. Have we all gone bonkers?

The good news is that becoming more aware of our habits, patterns and lifestyle choices can lead to making adjustments if necessary. My intention is not to make you feel bad. The key here is balance and re-prioritising. For example, no longer doing everything for everybody else, meaning you put yourself and your health at the top of the list.

You are of no use to your spouse or children if you are 'running on empty'. Our culture trains people to provide for their families. While this is admirable, if this is at the expense of your own physical and mental well-being, it can lead to all manner of negative consequences. So, work on having some balance, and invest in your self-care today.

CHAPTER FIVE

CATEGORY: FUN (LUCKY DIP)

Tip #38
Bitterness is Just for Lemons

Are you sweet or sour?

Have you ever seen the Facebook video of a baby tasting a lemon for the very first time? The poor baby's face makes for quite a funny picture when it sucks on a sour slice of lemon and it's hilarious. No wonder it's had millions of views. However, what's really cute for a baby isn't so adorable when we are in our 40s and beyond. Our reaction to feeling bitter is often far from sweet.

The Story of Mrs Crossman: The Sorceress of Sour

When I was a little boy in the 1970s, back when the absence of smartphones, computer games and the Internet meant we actually had to go outside to play, my sister and I lived next door to an old lady called Mrs Crossman. She lived alone, never had visitors and spent most of her time shouting at us children for making too much noise or playing on her grass and generally complaining if we breathed too loudly. Needless to say, we weren't close. I thought Mrs Crossman's name suited her well and hoped that I wouldn't be that mean when I was eventually her age.

Looking back, I've realised that she can only have been in her early 50s (and I'm 50 in three years). Panic!

Having had my fair share of disappointments, pain and failure, I now know how hard it is not to let life's challenges make us bitter (being unhappy about other people's happiness, resentful of other people's success and generally feeling like life has treated us cruelly). No wonder we see some elderly people who have a face like a slapped bottom.

So, here's the question: Is this how we want to feel? If not, is there something we can do to avoid this? In my personal experience and from coaching many people over the years, I've concluded that the best ways of overcoming sour-faceitis are:

1. Be aware of when and why you're feeling resentful. Is being aware enough? What can you do about it? I think it would be great to mention the importance of communication, for example. Also, that it's unavoidable to feel bitter or resentful as it's part of human nature but what you do about it is up to you.

2. Stop dwelling on the past. It's over. Find ways to let it go and move on. Give yourself one minute ruminating, snap your fingers and move on (literally). Go for a walk, get the Hoover out or do something that changes your focus.
3. Avoid focusing on what others are doing or achieving. Instead spend that energy on something more productive, something that makes you happy: a new project, a hobby, something that draws you out of yourself and may be of service to others.
4. Channel that negative energy into something positive. It's understandable to feel unhappy about past hurts or unfulfilled ambitions. The question is what do you do with those feelings? Why not harness that energy into something that turns your frown upside down?

Conclusion

When you notice the seeds of bitterness start to germinate, stop watering them. Instead sow seeds of optimism, hope, adventure, curiosity, playfulness and open-heartedness, and plant them in a nourishing environment. Invest in good friends, close family, an art class or a local community activity. Since choosing to focus on future goals, I've started to share my knowledge and desire to keep growing with others while trying new things and believing that the best is yet to come. This is something I have to practise on a daily basis and it does get easier over time. I'm now savouring the sweet nectar of making the best of mid-life rather than sucking on lemons. And you can too.

Why not list five things that you could do to turn bitter into better. Here's a couple of mine. Firstly, forgive others. Holding a grudge does more damage to me than them. And secondly: not apologising for myself by accepting my insecurities, sensitivities and failings.

1.

2.

3.

4.

5.

Tip #39
Fun is Fundamental

"A day without laughter is a day wasted."

– Charlie Chaplin

Of all the things that we need more of as we get older, maintaining a sense of humour is essential. I'm so grateful that my ability to find the funny side of things and seek out the silliness during challenging times has been an absolute life-saver for me-time and time again.

For me, nothing feels as good as uncontrollable laughter. It's pure joy and is by far the best medicine. There are so many reasons why having a good old giggle is amazing for us physically as well as emotionally. It quickly reduces pain and stress, it can instantly lighten your mood and it's an incredible way of letting go of pent-up anger and frustration.

The act of laughter helps to release endorphins (your body's feel-good chemicals) which promotes a delightful sense of well-being, calm and relaxation. Laughter decreases stress hormones, boosts your immune system, reduces tension and is actually good for your heart. Surprisingly, a good belly laugh can burn some calories too.

The impact on mental health is also dramatic. Cultivating a sense of fun is an extremely effective way of remaining optimistic and positive during challenging times. Humour helps to reduce anxiety, to see a different point of view, to get you out of your head, forget resentments and release inhibitions.

During a particularly messy break-up with a boyfriend, I went to a local Italian restaurant with a good friend. I ordered food in an attempt to cheer me up. I was so upset that when my meal arrived I decided to stick my entire face in the bowl of red-hot pasta (don't try this at home, guys) and burnt my forehead, nose and chin. This resulted in hysterical laughter from me and my friend and really helped to lighten the mood.

How to get more laughter in your life:

*Hang out with people who are funny, upbeat and positive.

*Do more fun activities like karaoke, pottery, naked mud wrestling. (Okay, maybe not pottery)

*Watch funny films and TV shows.

*Go to comedy shows.

*Spend more time with animals or children.

*Try new experiences. There's a lot of fun to be had when we are out of our comfort zone.

Why not schedule these into your diary to make sure you include plenty of laughter in your life? Feeling down can become a habit so we need a structure in place to lift us out of it.

Best of all, laughter is completely free, portable and it doesn't require any special equipment. We used to laugh all the time when we were children but as we get older the grown-up trials and tribulations of life can sadly result in laughter being a rare occurrence. Laughter is essential to a happy and healthy life so make it a top priority to have it be a part of your daily routine. An apple a day keeps the doctor away while laughter each day keeps sadness at bay.

The day laughter almost killed me.

There's been a lot of laughter in my life but there's only been one occasion when I laughed so much I truly thought I was going to die. I was in a bar with my best friend Amanda having a few drinks and when it came to paying our bill instead of using cash or our cards we attempted to try and settle it by using some bananas and apples we'd found in a nearby fruit bowl (you had to be there). For whatever reason, this struck us as the funniest thing in the world and minutes of hysterical laughter followed. Both my friend and I just could not stop laughing. It became almost worrying. We both couldn't breathe properly. It was and remains one of my most cherished memories. 25 years later I can still tap into the feeling and it never fails to make me feel happier.

What moments of laughter, joy and merriment can you tap into to guarantee your mood lifts? Write them down now!

____________ ____________ ____________ ____________

____________ ____________ ____________ ____________

____________ ____________ ____________ ____________

____________ ____________ ____________ ____________

Tip #40
Making Mundane Moments Magic

Just married the love of your life? Finally moved into the house of your dreams? Welcomed your first child into the world? If the answer is yes to one or all of these questions then may I wholeheartedly congratulate you. It's truly wonderful to celebrate these landmark occasions so crack open the champagne and get the bunting out. However, as we get older it can sometimes feel that there's less and less to be excited about. So many of life's significant milestones seem to occur between the ages of 18-35 that mid-life and beyond can often feel uneventful in comparison. Other than grandchildren, some of my older clients worry that there's a lack of things to look forward to.

As much as it's true that during our late teens, 20s and 30s we can witness many rites of passage, with a little creativity and shift in perspective, it's possible for us to create a wide variety of ways to inject some magic into our lives.

Jeff Olsen, in the fantastic book *The Slight Edge* teaches us that in order to have an enjoyable and rewarding older life we need to master the mundane to create magical moments. I love that concept!

When Life Gives You Lemons, Make Lemonade

Once upon a time, there were two friends, Kris and Dan, one of whom is a client of mine. They shared a flat and I learned from them that one Sunday morning they decided to have breakfast together but there was only some white bread and a bit of peanut butter in the fridge. Kris wasn't at all inspired so he simply spread the peanut butter on the bread while Dan toasted the bread, cut it into little squares and arranged it attractively on a special plate. He heated the peanut butter, added some hot chocolate powder to make a dipping sauce and, choosing a matching cup and saucer, placed his breakfast on a stylish wooden tray while Kris used his hand as a plate. The moral of this story is: It's not always what you have, it's what you do with it.

Life, as we get older, can sometimes feel exceedingly hum-drum. Days, weeks, months and years can seem like one big blur unless we can learn to create magic moments out of the everyday. If we put our minds to it, we can create extraordinary events, anniversaries and celebrations out of the ordinary.

Here are some ideas to master the mundane.

*Celebrating friendships: Why not pick an annual 'friendiversary' with your most treasured friends and organise an outing or a day-trip?

*Reunions: Organise getting together with old school friends, university pals or ex-work colleagues.

*Family time: Watch less Netflix and play more board games together.

*Make the dull delightful: Wear a tiara while doing the dishes; dress up in your smartest clothes to take the bins out; have a picnic in your garden; make up a breakfast tray once a week with fresh flowers and lovely crockery; put on your favourite dance music to unload the dishwasher.

For years, I've been exploring ways of enjoying the everyday, of celebrating the casual. It's so easy to dismiss and overlook the small things in life in favour of the obvious 'stand out' moments in life: a job promotion, a wedding anniversary or an important birthday. Life's highlights may not naturally appear to come along as often when we enter the second half of our lives but the good news is we can create our own. I firmly believe that we write the story of our lives so choose to break the script, don't let the script break you.

Tip #41

Spice Up Your Life: Try New Things

They say a change is as good as a rest. We are, whether we like it or not, creatures of habit. Having a routine gives us stability; however, too much of the same things can leave a bland taste in our mouths.

One of the characteristics often associated with youth is a willingness to have new experiences, to explore what we haven't tried before without a great deal of thought or hesitation. As we reach our middle years and above, we tend to take fewer risks, stick to what we know and generally stay in our lane. We can eat the same breakfast each day, drive the exact same route to work and go to our local pub every Friday for years. As much as a degree of familiarity can give a warm, cosy glow, it can also stifle us from growing and spreading our wings. Life can become dull and monotonous if we only do what we've always done.

The story of Amanda and the tree:

I often share this old fable with clients about an author called Amanda. She lived in a little cottage in the middle of the woods surrounded by beautiful trees of all shapes, sizes and ages. There was one tree, in particular, that was Amanda's absolute favourite: a tall, majestic oak tree. Each day, weather permitting, she would sit under this tree to write her stories. One day, she heard a voice say, "Hello, Amanda". To her surprise, it was the oak tree talking. "I have a question for you. Why do people stop growing when trees never stop?" Amanda, for once, was lost for words.

The truth is, in order to have a happy, dynamic and adventurous older life we need to keep growing, keep trying new things and make a conscious effort to step out of our comfort zones. All too often we put a lid on how much we grow and sometimes we suffer as a result.

I'm not suggesting you make drastic changes. If you want to sell your house and all your belongings to travel the world, then go ahead. However, we can start small by simply mixing things up a bit.

> *"Stay curious. Keep learning and keep growing. And always strive to be more interested than interesting."*
>
> – Jane Fonda

Here are some ideas for mixing things up.

*Try a different breakfast cereal.
*Take another route to work.
*Eat lunch somewhere you've not been before.
*Try a hobby that you wouldn't normally consider.
*Book a holiday somewhere you've never visited.
*Listen to a genre of music that's not your usual choice.
*Taste a fruit or vegetable you haven't eaten before.

*Wear a colour that you would usually run a mile from.
*Keep learning: Knowledge doesn't stop when we leave school.

There are hundreds of simple, free ways to keep life interesting. If we stick to only eating the exact same food for 30 years we will never experience all the other flavours.

When we expand our range of experiences, we literally broaden our horizons. To thrive rather than survive our older years. By dipping our toes into the pool of the new, the different and the unfamiliar, we can add a sparkle to our lives and inspire curiosity, playfulness, spontaneity and joie de vivre.

Tip #42
Flight or Fight?

There's an old wives' tale, that may even be true, about a scientist who conducted an experiment by placing fleas in a glass jar. Once inside they immediately jumped out again. Returning the fleas back into the jar he then placed a glass lid over the top. The jumping fleas hit the glass lid and fell back down into the jar. This continued for a while until the fleas became used to the glass lid being there and began jumping slightly below the lid to avoid hitting it. The scientist then removed the glass lid and discovered that the fleas had been conditioned not to jump beyond the height of the lid even when the lid was removed.

What does this experiment teach us? How often do we stop reaching for the things we want in life because of past disappointments, dejections and failures? Sadly, most people are conditioned to not jump so high as a result of negative experiences. It's human nature to avoid discomfort and danger. It's in our DNA and has helped us survive as a species; however, it can make us play small and stay safely in our comfort zones.

Despite the fact that the lid has been removed we remain trapped even though we are, in fact, free. The consequence of this is that we can become passive, fearful and anxious about taking action that may result in uncertainty, challenges or failure.

We can become so scared of life that we no longer take risks and our horizons become narrower and narrower. So, what's the answer? For me, the solution has been finding my fight. Within each and every one of us, there's a superhero just dying to get out. If there are things you really want to do – get healthier, improve your fitness, travel, start a new business or improve a relationship – then you need to get your magic boxing gloves on.

We're all so much more powerful than we can ever know. All we need to do is to come out of the shadows, stand tall and get ready to fight for what we want.

For me, everything changed when I read Bronnie Ware's incredible book *The Top Five Regrets of the Dying*. This is a moving and inspiring account of Bronnie's experiences of caring for terminally ill people. According to her, the number one regret in people who are dying is regret itself. So many of us are so scared of failure that we never even try. Reading this book was a turning point for me. I decided then and there to be courageous and jump out of my own glass jar to freedom. I would rather experience the pain of spectacular failure than the agony of regret any day. I can't recommend this book highly enough. If you need a giant boost of motivation, encouragement or even a kick up the backside then order it today.

In your own life can you think of examples of times when you've been thumped about by life so much that you're now contemplating giving up on your hopes and dreams? If so, then please consider this:

> *"An arrow can only be shot by pulling it backwards. When life is dragging you back with difficulties, it means it's going to launch you into something great. So just focus and keep aiming."*
>
> – Source unknown

Tip #43
You Are Enough

We live in a world where there is so much pressure to constantly prove ourselves. Everywhere we look there are messages to do more, be better and work harder. It can be exhausting. We have a culture of dissatisfaction: We aren't slim enough, muscular enough, attractive enough, wealthy enough, productive enough – the list is literally endless. God forbid that we are actually content and satisfied with who we are. No wonder all this striving is driving people mad. It can seem positively shocking if someone is genuinely happy in themselves as they are.

I'm all for making changes, to keep improving and growing but not if we feel we aren't already perfect in our imperfections. This is especially relevant as we get older: The pressure to stay slim, not age, be a better parent/spouse/employee can feel overwhelming and lead to a mid-life crisis if we aren't careful.

What do you say to yourself about yourself? Be honest! Are you continually chastising yourself for not being good enough? Sadly, for most people, the answer is yes. As human beings, we all want the same things: love, respect, acceptance, to belong, to feel special and wanted, and a desire to be seen and heard. It's how we go about getting these things that is the question.

For me, it's all about understanding that our worth isn't bound up in anything we do but instead in who we are. This is easier said than done. We aren't encouraged to like ourselves. Self-love can be viewed as narcissistic; accepting and appreciating ourselves as vanity. Not working night and day to prove ourselves can be viewed as lazy.

It's time to take a stand. What a waste of a life to refuse to believe we are enough just as we are. Now that doesn't mean we'll sit around feeling self-satisfied all day. Rather, when we truly accept we have nothing to prove to anyone we get to choose what we'd like to explore. So many people are trying so hard to be good enough, to impress others, to feel better about themselves because deep down they feel they simply don't measure up.

Here's what I recommend: Go to the mirror and say, "I am enough" ten times a day. It may sound quirky but it works. It really helps to reduce the enormous pressure we put on ourselves. We can still pursue our goals. We can still be ambitious. We can still strive to make improvements to our lives. Yet, we can do so from a position of strength.

Here are some affirmations to help you get more in touch with your inner gorgeousness.

*I like myself exactly as I am. I plan to lose some weight/get fitter/eat better but only as a consequence of deep self-respect and acceptance.

*I'm fabulous because I'm fabulous. I don't need a reason or any evidence to feel wonderful about myself.

*I treat myself with kindness. I'm my own cheerleader. I encourage myself rather than constantly beat myself up with a stick.

*I know my worth is all about who I am instead of what I do.

*I'm perfect as I am. I'm happy to make changes to my health and fitness because I really value myself as I am right now.

Remember: You are enough, you are enough, you are enough. You have nothing to prove to anyone; you are free to respect yourself exactly as you are, so get out there and go make what you want happen.

Tip #44

It's Not Too Late, The Best is Yet to Come

A few years ago, I had a meeting with a business consultant. I was feeling I hadn't quite found my voice, was in the midst of rebranding and was in severe need of some professional advice. In all, we had three meetings to discuss what the essence of my business was. I had gone into the process fairly convinced that my future path lay in the anti-ageing industry and came away with a very different focus entirely.

It was fascinating to discover that what lay underneath everything I did was the belief that it's never too late to be healthier and happier. That age needn't be a barrier to achieving our hopes and dreams.

We live in a youth-obsessed culture where, as teenagers, we are pressured into deciding what we want to do for the rest of our lives. At 18, I wanted to be Madonna's backing dancer. In 1989, in a sleepy village in Cornwall, England, my career advisor wasn't particularly optimistic or encouraging about my showbiz aspirations.

It wasn't until my early 40s that I finally discovered what I wanted to do when I grow up.

If you sometimes feel that it's too late for you to try a

new career or business, I'm delighted to inform you that it's not. We live in a technological age where there are extraordinary opportunities to create something uniquely yours with access to millions of people through the World Wide Web and social media.

Here are some inspiring examples of people who achieved extraordinary things over the age of 40:

Charles Darwin was 50 when he published *On the Origin of Species* in 1859.

Martha Stewart was 41 when she published her first book, *Entertaining,* and she launched *Martha Stewart Living* aged 48.

Samuel L. Jackson was 46 before he got his 'lucky' break starring alongside John Travolta in *Pulp Fiction*.

Ray Croc was in his 50s before he bought the first McDonald's in 1961.

Vera Wang was first known as an accomplished figure skater and a fashion editor before deciding at 40 that she wanted to be a designer and opened her first bridal boutique the following year.

We need more positive role-models of older people taking risks, having adventures and stepping out of their comfort zone. It's time for us mid-lifers to become more visible. As a global population, we are all living longer and rather than feeling we are hurtling towards downhill oblivion past 40, how about choosing to ramp things up and blast off into uncharted territory during our 'second act'?

It's so easy to feel that our best days are behind us and reminisce about 'the good old days', well here's something to rock your world: These are the good old days. Right here, right now.

Is there something you've always wanted to try? A business idea or adventure that you've told yourself you're too old to pursue? As we get older the temptation is to stick with what we know and play it safe. I know from my own experience that true happiness exists outside our comfort zones. Four years ago, I had never even used Facebook. However, by taking little steps I slowly learnt lots of new skills, so you can too. Never underestimate the magic that occurs when you decide to be courageous enough to begin something new. It can be really frightening but believe me it's so worth it. When you're growing as a person you are truly alive. So, to avoid shrinking (emotionally as well as physically) as you age, make a decision today to create the future you want because fear is temporary, regret is forever.

"It's never too late to be what you might have been."

– George Elliot

Tip #45
How to Be Truly Gorgeous

As The Gorgeousness Coach, I help people to look and feel gorgeous inside and out.

When you take care of the exterior – food, fitness, skin care, fashion, lifestyle – it has a very positive impact on your confidence and self-esteem. The opposite is also true: When you love and respect yourself, you naturally take better care of yourself. Make sense?

So many people feel they should eat less and exercise more. This can feel like a chore or an obligation and not particularly enjoyable. However, when you accept how fabulous you are you'll naturally want to take incredible care of yourself. Weight loss, getting fitter and looking more attractive are simply side-effects of choosing to value yourself and are not goals in themselves.

What makes someone beautiful anyway? Individuals who've won the genetic lottery and have appealing physical attributes are not necessarily beautiful. For me, the most attractive people I've ever met are those who are really comfortable in their own skin and they don't apologise for who they are but instead fully embrace themselves, flaws and all.

"Beauty begins the moment you decide to be yourself."

– Coco Chanel

Don't get me wrong, I like a handsome or pretty face as much as the next person but, for me, true gorgeousness is having a playful, fun, kind and curious attitude. So why not be your own kind of beautiful? You don't have to conform to any stereotype. Making the most of your appearance is ideally an expression of high self-worth. It's the gift you give to yourself first and then to others.

Sadly, it seems that most of the fun has disappeared from the messages we hear about physical and emotional wellness. I'm on a mission to bring back the laughter. Who's up for actually enjoying the journey?

If we are frightened, bullied or guilt-tripped into lifestyle changes, most of us will resist like mad. Rather than the finger-pointing "you should" approach I greatly prefer a "let's do it together" philosophy by finding creative, imaginative and humorous ways to look and feel your best.

IF YOU
CAN'T BE
GOOD, BE
gorgeous
BECAUSE
YOU'RE TOO
GLAM TO
GIVE A DAMN
tristanlee

Tip #46
Ageing is Inevitable, Misery is Optional: Making the Most of Getting Older

There is a strict rule every year when it's my cousin's birthday: Do not mention it. She'll happily accept discreet presents (wrapped in plain paper) but absolutely no cards or singing Happy Birthday. To be reminded of another passing year is too much for her. Despite looking good for her age, she decided about six years ago to simply stop celebrating her birthday so she'll be forever 48.

> *"We don't stop playing because we grow old, we grow old because we stop playing."*
>
> – George Bernard Shaw

For many of us, the thought of getting older can fill us with dread and horror. In our youth-obsessed culture, ageing is viewed as a terrible affliction to be avoided at all costs. Cosmetic surgery is now a multi-billion-pound industry and that can, in some cases, lead to people attempting to erase every trace of the passage of time.

No-one wants to age but I believe that there is a massive distinction between anti-ageing and ageing well. I'm not at all interested in fighting the ageing process (that would be a losing battle) but these days there's so much we can do to age with attitude which has as much to do with feelings as it does with how we look.

Everyone is getting older, it's not personal. Brad Pitt, Angelina Jolie and other physically beautiful people aren't exempt from this process. It's just what happens. Deal with it.

We cannot control the fact that we are all ageing but we can have a huge impact on how we age: Regular exercise, eating healthy food, remaining curious, being adventurous, surrounding ourselves with positive people, maintaining good friendships, trying new things and having fun are just a few of the ways we can look and feel gorgeous during the second act of our lives. It does take an effort to stay physically and emotionally healthy but the rewards are so worthwhile.

Since time began, people have been born, aged and died and it looks like that's a trend that will continue for the time being so to ignore and resist this fact is like denying the world is round. There are plenty of people who deny the cycle of life so here's my advice...don't be one of them. Do whatever you can to accept and make the most of being alive.

For me, every birthday is a celebration that I'm still here. We are all living longer so mid-life is really just that: the halfway point, the second half, the time when we have the opportunity to put into practice all the lessons we've learnt in our first act.

So be loud and proud each year when your birthday comes around. To shake our fists at our inevitable demise is such a waste of time, but to embrace and make the most of life, our wrinkles and sagging boobs is a far better goal to aim for. There are many benefits that ageing can bring such as growing wisdom, the ability to let things go more easily and a firm commitment to keeping the stress out of your life.

Ageing and misery aren't synonymous. I fully intend to have the best 'second half' imaginable. I'll be wearing feather boas in my senior living community. By having a proactive approach to taking care of our physical and emotional needs (starting right now), we are significantly more likely to be healthy and happy in our 40s, 50s, 60s and beyond. My belief is that the more of us who are visibly having fun and living full, exciting and purposeful lives as we get older, the more of us can, over time, start to change attitudes to ageing. Is this a challenge you are up for?

Oh, and if you see my cousin Laura on the 6th November don't forget to wish her "Happy Birthday!" :-)

Tip #47

Ageing with Attitude

Some folks can hold their breath for a long time, others can do celebrity impersonations but my party piece has always been that I look young for my age. Despite the fact that I'm 47 years old, when people learn about this when I'm out and about celebrating my birthday, they steadfastly refuse to accept it (See for yourself? Check out www.tristanlee.com/age)

I'm not a proponent of anti-ageing. Instead I'm a fan of pro-health, pro-youthfulness and ageing well inside and out. For me, looking younger is a pleasant side effect of taking great care of myself, not the goal.

People often ask me how I've managed to maintain my 'boyish' looks, so...

Here are my top five 'secrets' to ageing well:

1. Sun protection: My number one tip for looking young and slowing down the ageing process is to protect yourself from the damaging effects of UV exposure. None of us desire to have lots of wrinkles so be sure not to let the sun have too much opportunity to cause the damage that it is capable of. Give it half a chance and it will continue to break down the collagen and elastin which helps to keep the skin looking firm and

soft. Using a daily moisturiser containing SPF on your face, neck and hands is a sure-fire way of protecting those areas that are vulnerable to sun exposure. Use it every day, even in winter for maximum results.

2. Skincare: Of all our organs, your skin is the biggest and as such it's essential to keep it in tip-top condition. Both your face and body need to be looked after properly. Both men and women have certainly got better at taking care of their complexions but more often than not they completely neglect their skin from the neck down. By cleansing your entire body each day your skin will look gorgeous and smooth. Taking care of your skin not only helps you look good and feel great, it also helps you look your best for longer.

3. Water and Nutrition: If we want to age well then it really helps to understand that ultimately looking good is an inside job. It surprises me that some people are very particular about their grooming and beauty routines but eat terribly. You are what you eat and what you put in your body shows itself on the outside through your appearance and the state of your complexion. So, drinking plenty of water and eating a healthy diet will do wonders for your appearance. All the moisturiser in the world counts for nothing if you're constantly shovelling junk food in your mouth. Poor quality foods, including sugar-laden, fat-

drenched and salt-rich processed products, age the skin prematurely. Fresh fruit, vegetables as well as foods high in antioxidants have been proven to slow down the ageing process. You wouldn't put inferior fuel in your car so don't put bad fuel in your body. It goes without saying that excessive alcohol consumption and smoking both dramatically accelerate the ageing process.

4. Exercise: Not only will exercise improve the shape of your body but it will also do wonders for your self-esteem. Even moderate levels of exercise have been found to have a significant impact on both our physical health and state of mind. Slim, fit bodies are synonymous with youth and vitality. Any activity that keeps the body in shape, that promotes flexibility, increases circulation and improves bone and muscle density should be incorporated into your life.

5. Lifestyle: Stress, lack of sleep and pollution all contribute to us ageing before our time. Therefore, I encourage us all to invest in me-time. A holistic approach to health and wellbeing is needed in order to live a happy, balanced life. So many people put themselves at the bottom of the list. If you're a busy husband, wife, dad or mum, you're of no use to anyone if you don't take care of yourself. If you want to age well, then prioritise opportunities to

relax and unwind. Allocate time for these and put them in your diary. The minutiae that we distract ourselves with such as tidying the cupboards, dusting your royal thimble collection, reorganising your sock draw and watching cat videos can wait – your health shouldn't play second fiddle. Start to prioritise YOU and your health.

Conclusion

You can't stop nature taking its course but you can certainly put the brakes on and slow down the process. We live in a culture that is obsessed with youth; however, my emphasis is not on fighting getting older – far from it.

In fact, I think we should celebrate that we've made it this far. My focus is on looking and feeling my best for as long as I can and having fun doing it by not losing my sense of humour on this subject. I haven't got a problem with ageing but I'm not a fan of sullen complexions, poor diets and unfit physiques. Being passionate, playful and energetic with a zest for life beats a wrinkle-free face any day. Genes do play a role in the ageing process but you can make a massive difference through the lifestyle choices you make.

IT'S BEEN FUN!

Congratulations, you've made it. You've got to the end. Phew! Give yourself a well-deserved round of applause. How was it for you?

I hope you've learnt something new, that you've had a laugh and feel motivated to get stuck in. Whether you simply want to make a couple of small changes or are interested in a complete health and wellbeing overhaul, I hope the hints and tips contained in this book will encourage you to take the necessary steps.

It isn't selfish to care about your appearance and your health. In fact, the opposite is true because when you take care of yourself, everyone around you benefits.

I know how amazing you can feel by putting aside some time to look after yourself. If you don't believe me, try it. The greatest gift we can give our significant other, family and friends, is to do all we can to look after ourselves. We aren't much use to our nearest and dearest if we neglect our own health.

Taking pride in your appearance is great for your mental health. Our mid-life years can be an exciting yet challenging time so if I can help to make this process more enjoyable and a little less stressful then I'll be a happy ginger. By getting started now, you'll establish good lifestyle habits which will set you up to look better and be happier for the rest of your life.

We have explored many topics in this book and I'm certainly not expecting you to do everything at once. It has taken me a long time to develop my routine so start with something simple like using face wash and build this up with other healthy habits over time. Even if you take on board just one new habit each week, I can guarantee you'll be thrilled with the results you see.

So, the lesson is clear: Look after yourself now and have the health and vitality to spend many happy years with those you love.

It's never too late to start, no matter what your age. There are 168 hours in a week, so prioritising and planning to spend just three or four of them engaging in physical activity is very achievable.

Spending a bit more time reading food labels, reducing sugar consumption and eating less processed food is a loving thing to do. Eating real food instead of junk food, drinking water rather than fizzy drinks are also loving things to do. All that's required is a change of mind-set and consideration of the bigger picture.

How do you want to look and feel ten years from now? Start taking small steps today to improve your health and fitness, not just for yourself but also for those you love and who love you because...you're worth it.

GET IN TOUCH

This is just the beginning. I'd love to hear from you if you have any questions, comments or would like some more information on my one-to-one coaching packages. Please get in touch:

1. Email: tristan@tristanlee.com
2. Facebook page: Tristan Lee – facebook.com/realtristanlee
3. Twitter/Instagram: @realtristanlee

I also have a private, free Facebook group called 'Tristan's Gorgeousness Gang' for VIP, exclusive content on food, fitness and feeling fabulous. If you want to be a part of this fun and friendly community, please simply send a request to join by going to www.tristansgorgeousnessgang.co.uk

Can implementing the tips and hints in this book change your life? Well, it can certainly help you on the road to valuing yourself, looking and feeling more gorgeous, as well as gaining an increased respect for your physical and emotional health.

So, my dear readers, I wish you every success. Go forth and may the moisturiser be with you.

Tristan :-)
The Gorgeousness Coach

TESTIMONIALS ABOUT THE AUTHOR

"Tristan's natural overdose of empathy comes through in everything he does. When working one-to-one with him, he has only ever supported changes from my current and historical dangerously unhealthy lifestyle, helping me gently but successfully towards a healthier future.

I feel better and in my opinion look better already. Whilst I fear I've left it too late to emulate Tristan's youthful good looks, I know that I am track for feeling better as I approach the end of my forties, than I did at the end of my thirties.

I've worked with various people before to help me to feel better. Tristan's advice stands out as it is practical, simple and effective, all delivered with immense kindness. Thank you Tristan!"
Stefan Thomas, Speaker and Author, 48 and a half, Oxfordshire

"I always look forward to watching Tristan's Facebook videos. He makes everything simple - with sensible, easy to follow advice. His recipes and food advice are second to none - and they just work!

Tristan has a very infectious laugh which makes his delivery fun and easy to listen to.

I am very lucky to not look my age, but I am constantly looking for good advice and also hints and tips on skin preparations to look the best I can, keeping fit and healthy.

Following Tristan's advice, I now have a personal trainer helping me with my fitness routine, I am making better food choices and eating healthier than ever, and I have been using the skin preparations he has recommended."
Malcolm Wolpert, 69, London

"Tristan's posts have inspired me to cook more and eat nutrient dense food that is so easy to make and that feels and tastes SO great! I love his approach to life - looking after food, fitness and feelings. I was already eating healthily but his food is on another level. I have felt encouraged to bring more fitness into my life in a way that works for me and I am delighted that someone in this field is at last looking at the whole and including the importance of our feelings and attitude in life as part of our fitness."
Amanda Jayne, 47, Author of 'Close Encounters of the Travelling Kind', Los Angeles, USA

"I have learnt so much from Tristan, making lots of changes with my healthy eating and skin care regime. He really knows his stuff but also makes everything fun."
Sarah Protheroe, 37, South Wales

"Tristan's content is informative, practical, yet very entertaining. He always provides small tangible steps, easy to implement into my busy life.

His recipes are inspiring, healthy and nutritious which has turned my simple plating into a food-styling journey. He has been instrumental in my self-love and self-care journey due to the simplicity, value for money and knowledge I gained."
Katarzyna Stomska, 34, Poland

"I follow Tristan on all his social media channels and I have been particularly interested in his healthy eating tips and ideas. Having taken them on board and cut out many unhealthy snacks, some recent health tests that I have regularly are the best they have ever been."
Jonathan Horswell, Norfolk

"Tristan gives me the hope and belief that whilst I'm growing older I can still look, feel and do everything that I've been doing since I was a teenager. When I wake up in the morning the first thing I do is go on social media and 'like' Tristan's posts - he gives me motivation for the day ahead."
Ian Stewart, 38, Luton, Bedfordshire

"What I LOVE about Tristan's social media, and all his content, is the fun, engaging and simple way that he explains the advice he gives out, and clearly takes himself.

Following his journey on social media over the years has put him right up (doesn't make sense) as THE guy to follow for looking good and feeling great - what a legend.

Invest in yourself and make it fun while you do it. Enjoy!"
Graham Todd, Warwick

"I can honestly say I look forward to his posts about health and happiness every day. I love Tristan's no-nonsense but non-judgemental approach towards his mission and life. His attitude is infectious!"
Geraint Jones, Cardiff, Wales

"I attended my first event with Tristan a year ago. I didn't know what to expect but I was blown away with how he made me feel. He made me realise I am worthy of taking time out for myself and it's not selfish. I have since become a client on a one-to-one basis."
Paula Butcher, 52, Kent

"Tristan has taught me that living healthily and becoming the most gorgeous version of myself isn't simply luck. He's helped me positively transform the way in which I approach what I eat and how I work out. It's one of the best things I could've done for myself. It's never too late to begin working towards the best you. Thank you, Tristan!"
Laurence Snow, 19, Folkestone, Kent

"Tristan has had a huge impact on not only my life, but also that of my children in the last year. Whether it's making healthy snacks or his Facebook Live videos where he tackles our perception of ourselves and offers tips to improve our quality of life; to business tips on how to create that all important positive first impression, Tristan delivers his messages in a unique and humorous style which is fully inclusive. He adds a dose of daily sparkle to our lives and is genuinely one of the most caring and generous people I've ever met!"
Vanessa O'Shea, Andover, Hampshire

"Tristan exudes warmth, kindness and enthusiasm, and he always looks AMAZING!

I love seeing his daily posts and learning from someone who is completely and utterly gorgeous inside and out. His ideas are inspired but achievable for anyone.

As well as his general gorgeousness, he is hilariously funny and has the world's best cheekbones."
Anna May, 42, Wiltshire

"I read all you portray. I love your tips on health, I follow all your recipes and I love your perspective and positivity. You make it sound so easy to turn your life around in simple ways, which I personally agree with, and feel people should follow you on social media to achieve everything you want."
Jenny Thomas, 64, Bodmin, Cornwall

"I've been following Tristan on Facebook since the day he started and every day I see inspirational messages, quotes and food ideas which I love. I've also attended one of Tristan's workshops recently which was really inspiring, showing you how to change small things within your life which will make huge life changes for you.

I would recommend Tristan to anyone, however healthy, fit or old they are!"
Josh Hollands, 23, Manilva, Spain

"Tristan has made an extremely important impact on my life by being so positive about every aspect of life. The most important one being to always be yourself and stop trying to please others. I feel this is a strong message to get across to so many people who have always tried to please but never get anything back.

He is always there every morning with wonderful suggestions and helping people with what to think about, rather than telling them what to think. His messages and poignant life quotes truly make people think about what they need to change.

From a lifestyle point of view, he makes such an impact with his healthy, creative recipes which are easy to follow, as well as being quick to make.

His inspiring fitness regime speaks for itself. I mean, look at that skin, that hair and that physique - he is

living proof that you are what you eat, which cannot fail to promote a healthy lifestyle to keep youthful looks and a healthy body inside and out. Thanks for making a difference."
Jackie Travers, Dancer and TV Presenter, 63, London

"Tristan's videos and photos of what's he's made and is just about to eat are the highlight of my Facebook newsfeed!

I started following him a couple of years ago and can honestly say dropping a stone in weight has been due to following his advice on intermittent fasting and smarter food choices: he makes it interesting and fun!

He's a really positive influence and can laugh at himself. Love him!"
Marsha Gomez, London

"Working on a one-to-one basis with Tristan has been life-changing, and I don't say that lightly.

In-between running a company and balancing a fast-paced life, I had very little time for myself, my health or my wellbeing. However, working with Tristan has transformed this area of my life, leading to drastic changes in nutrition, a rekindled love of cooking, great weight-loss results and an all-round happier life, with a renewed work-life balance.

Tristan has helped me realise my inner potential, and

our weekly coaching calls help keep me on-track and accountable, by embracing that it's not about 'being perfect', but about being consistent and forgiving yourself the occasional slip.

I would recommend Tristan to anyone who is serious about making a positive change in their life, whether that's weight loss, fitness, eating well or feeling great. I have never met a more compassionate, motivating and supportive person, and I am eternally grateful for his support and look forward to many more years working together."
Dan Debnam, 28, Casares, Spain

"I'm a HUGE fan of Tristan Lee for his very welcome dose of daily fun and inspiration. Not to mention the live videos full of marvellous tips delivered with such lightness and humour. I can't wait for the book!"
Claudia Sorrentino, 52, Padova, Italy

"Tristan's thoughtful, inspiring and motivating social media content comes from a place of genuine care for other people, and a true desire to help people achieve their personal health, fitness and self-care goals.

Personally, I adore his encouragement for people to accept themselves the way they are, and to embrace making small steps on a daily basis towards their personal goals. He's helped me on a journey to stop beating myself up on a daily basis, and start to accept that it's actually okay to be me.

Plus he's gorgeous and hilarious too!"
Bev Blackburn, 35, Halifax